Naija No Dey Carry Last!

Praise for Naija No Dey Carry Last

"Hilarious... This is not absurdity, this is not satire, this is not camp. It is a strong concoction of the three served with a face so straight many will take it as serious and rally behind him for his earnest prescriptions on the Nigerian problem."
—Kingwa Kamencu.

"For several years, Pius Adesanmi has been one of Nigeria's most prolific satirists. 'Naija No Dey Carry Last' is a collection of writings, written mostly between 2008 and 2010, which takes aim at various public figures, from the late Umaru Yar'Adua to Goodluck Jonathan, Ikedi Ohakim, Farida Waziri, and many others. Adesanmi employs satire and Biblical metaphors to deliver scathing criticism of Nigerian politics and society.

Nigeria is one country where events are often so unbelievable, that they defy satirical treatment. Still, he manages to pull it off, and I heartily recommend 'Naija No Dey Carry Last' to anyone who wants to read about the issues and events concerning Nigeria's fourth attempt at democracy with a different twist."
—Chude Jideonwo.

"In this book, Pius Adesanmi delivers brilliant political satire with with his incredible skill at serving ridiculous fun. The artistic merit of Naija No Dey Carry Last lies in the freewheeling anarchic wit of blending cultural infusions and the Nigerian street language, without any loss of expression identity. Parresia offers everyone's favourite lampoonist in a book filled with irreverent, side-splitting read, that never fails to amuse."
—Bamidele Ademola-Olateju.

"One of the best decisions Pius Adesanmi has made in recent times is to publish all his contributions to Nigeria's socio-political development. He employed every literary missile in his arsenal to take on and effectively bring down a profligate government to her knees. That's how much power his writings carry.

Naija no dey carry last because Pius no gree carry last. Educating, riveting, captivating, thrilling and enthralling, Pius' mastery of African Literature and deployment of anecdotes we all can relate to will make you eagerly move on to the next word, flip to the next page, roar with laughter or even cry.

No one does intellection on Naija issues better than Pius Adesanmi. Everyone should get a copy of Naija No Dey Carry Last."
—Petra Akinti Onyegbule.

"Pius Adesanmi's *Naija No Dey Carry Last* is a treasure of pleasures, a gem of a book. Adesanmi is a prodigious writer and deep thinker whose essays exude vigorous intelligence, rare insight and a devastating wit. The essays in this peerless collection are irreverent, evocative, mind-expanding, and highly entertaining. This kaleidoscopic, take-no-prisoner's romp through the vital social, cultural and political issues of Nigeria will thrill, inform and transform you. I urge you to read and reread this terrific, capacious book—and then tell all your friends about it."
—Okey Ndibe (author of the novels *Arrows of Rain* and *Foreign Gods, Inc.*)

"The essence of Pius Adesanmi's public commentary is not in what he says but how he says it: a fluency of thought and language, rich in wit and humour – very rare combination that however reflects the writer's ebullience; his depth of conviction, fertile imagination and arduous cognition. Adesanmi's robust intervention in national discourse has taught us a new diction in 'public intellectualism' – a pleasurable reading, reflection on, and presentation of the many farcical, often sub-intelligent reasoning and actions of the elites, especially rulers to whom good, purposeful leadership is an anathema. In this volume, our national conversation is truly enriched…"
—Jahman Anikulapo, journalist and culture advocate.

This collection, *"Naija No Dey Carry Last",* is a clear testimony to why Pius Adesanmi commands attention as one of the most profound and thought-provoking essayists of our generation, making it a worthwhile read for anyone interested in seeking a better understanding of Nigeria and Nigerians. While most of the offerings were published at different times during a momentous period in our nation's history, reading them all at once, one is struck by the author's deployment of wit and humour to tell a compelling story that would make readers laugh and cry about our beloved country.
—**Olusegun Adeniyi**

"The point of this collection of satirical pieces, covering a handful of years from Nigeria's recent history, is that the country repeats itself endlessly as farce. In piece after satirical piece we're given a privileged glimpse of Africa's largest circus stage, filled with a cast of clowns whose genius lies in make biting satire feel like breaking news. And yet with all their talent, none can overshadow the biggest star of the production: Déjà Vu. *Naija No Dey Carry Last* is an immensely entertaining show of words: paeans, parables, plays and epistles; Pius Adesanmi does such a fine job one could easily get away with re-titling it: *Pius No Dey Carry Last!"*
—Tolu Ogunlesi, *West Africa Editor, The Africa Report.*

"Whether he's ruminating on government incompetence or taking a dig at the ineptness of some of our leaders, Pius
Adesanmi's unapologetic, searing wit makes us laugh and cry. We laugh because his take on issues is genuinely funny; we cry because our leaders are genuinely funny. Adesanmi is the Nigerian god of satire and here's his book of lamentations!"
—Lola Shoneyin, *author of The Secret Lives of baba Segi's Wives.*

"The Nigerian writers team in a relay should field Pius Adesanmi in final leg to do what he does in this collection: to pick up sundry fallen batons (in the tradition of men who never say 'no comment') and to run the length of his essays with panache, feisty energy, and the burst of insight that wins agreement."
—**Chuma Nwokolo, publisher of African Writing Journal, author of The Ghost of Sani Abacha.**

Naija No Dey Carry Last!

Thoughts on a Nation in Progress

PIUS ADESANMI

origami

PREMIUM TIMES Books

ISBN: 978-151-752-30-53

First Published in Nigeria by Parrésia Publishers Ltd.
34, Allen Avenue, Ikeja, Lagos
0815 458 2178
www.parresia.com.ng

For
Premium Times Books
53, Mambolo Street,
Wuse Zone 2, Abuja.
info@premiumtimesng.com

National Library of Nigeria Cataloguing-in-Publication Data.

Origami Books
An Imprint of Parrésia Publishers Ltd.
34, Allen Avenue, Ikeja, Lagos
0815 458 2178
www.parresia.com.ng

Printed and Bound in Nigeria by Parrésia Press

Dedication

For Oluwadamilare Adesanmi and Oluwatise Adesanmi… the patter of your little feet in my study provided musical accompaniment to the writing of many of these essays.

For the habitués of my Facebook wall, who have enriched and enlarged my world since I turned that space into a public classroom.

Table of Contents

Part One:
Naija no dey Carry Last

Part Two:
In the Beginning was the Word

Part Three:
Open Letters to Godot

Part Four:
All the World's a Stage

Note to the Reader

The essays in each section of this book have been arranged chronologically, in the order in which they were published. Because the author's desire remains to preserve memories of the subject matters they treat, no revisions have been undertaken. The essays have been reproduced in their original form.

PREFACE

The Price of Laughter

I was supposed to have submitted this manuscript to my publisher long before I eventually did. Writing being a strange profession, the written text often communicates moods and feelings to its producer in a language exclusive to both of them. Often, a manuscript tells its maker: never submit today what you can submit tomorrow – or even better, next week. The outside world calls it procrastination. The writer tells himself that it is a necessary delay to achieve perfection. A chapter could do with more honing; a sentence is not quite what it ought to be; a nuance is missing somewhere; a punchline needs to be delivered more effectively. Can you achieve tomorrow's perfect manuscript if you submit it today?

Oh yes, I'll submit this work tomorrow. And tomorrow. And tomorrow. Eventually, I ran out of tomorrows and sent it off to my publisher in the wee hours of January 7, 2015. After clicking the send button on an email which put an end to endless revisions deferred till tomorrow, I made coffee and switched on the television. To CNN…!

And everything changed!

French satirical magazine, *Charlie Hebdo*, had been attacked by armed terrorists who wiped out a generation of French satirists, humorists, and cartoonists. The old argument between the Islamic world and boundary-pushing artists, writers, and intellectuals over the limits of humour, satire, and, I daresay, creativity, had been taken to a murderous conclusion by Islamist terrorists – fundamentalist traducers of the very faith they claim to profess.

And I had chosen the very day of the Paris attacks to submit my manuscript!

Laughter went on trial. Satire was put into a position where she had to defend her right to exist. As the world slowly recovered from the initial shock of the *Charlie Hebdo* massacre, global punditry went into overdrive: should satire and humour respect religion, culture, and other boundaries? When does satire go too far? When does satire transgress? Perhaps there are national traits of humour and satire which only cultural insiders and initiates could understand? Are *Charlie Hebdo's* risqué satirical riffs on Jesus Christ, the Prophet Mohammed, the Pope, Africans, and Black people harmless vistas of French humour whose meaning the rest of us, non-French, are unable to appreciate?

I have had my own share of grief and trauma for deploying satire as my principal mode of intervention in the national affairs of Nigeria. Because satire is an art, talent is obligatory. However, recourse to satire as a tool for reflection on national issues goes beyond talent. It is a political decision. I decided to write satire because I felt a political urgency to communicate with a wide national audience in a country with a perverse hostility to intellectual depth and the written word: consequences of decades of elite assault on education and its associated values. In a country where a seven hundred-word analytical opinion article written in straightforward English always risks hostile dismissal as "*dogon turenchi*", "big grammar", "words without action" by an infinitesimal fragment of a public which dares to read anything beyond a paragraph, how do you connect?

I took a political decision to connect via laughter. Nigerians love to laugh. Self-deprecating humour of the beer parlour variety is a national pastime. It is not for nothing that a spurious study in Europe famously described Nigerians as the happiest people on earth. I started to write satire as a major part of an evolving career as a public intellectual in 2008. If it took laughter to get people to reflect seriously on the abject condition of our country and our lives, so be it!

Many of the essays in this collection went viral and the consequent attacks and threats against me have been vicious. Satire, a genre I resorted to out of a perceived national hostility to the mental and intellectual exertions required to engage a straightforward essay, has proven to be a much trickier business in the said anti-intellectual context. I have been savaged by literalist readers and nuanced misreaders alike. The Onaiyekan memos—a critique of the political class' disdain of speakers of truth to power like John Cardinal Onaiyekan—drew the ire of a large segment of the Catholic faithful. A Reverend Father wrote a long rejoinder in a national newspaper, pouring invectives on me for daring to criticise the Cardinal. The Cardinal's London-based younger brother made frantic efforts on social media to explain to the Catholic faithful that my essay was, in fact, a satirical piece written in support of his brother.

There has also been a second dilemma over my choice of satire as a medium of communication with the Nigerian public. The issues addressed via laughter in these essays touch on the fundamental problems of *project nationhood*. The intention is to induce serious critical reflection on such issues with a view to envisioning enduring solutions. I write satire that Nigeria may wake up and deliver on her promise and potential. However, over the years, I have had to get used to a situation in which the medium overwhelms the message. Those who do not fall prey to the dangers of literalist interpretation of satire have often fallen for the allure of laughter over reflection. As many of these essays went viral online, I would receive hundreds of fan mail from Nigerians at home and in the Diaspora praising my "talent and genius" and thanking me for making them laugh so hard, thereby offering an escape from the depressing condition of Nigeria.

But these satires are written to make you engage critically with the depressing condition of Nigeria!

These essays were published between 2008 and 2014 in my principal media of syndication as a columnist: *Sahara Reporters*, *Nigeria Village Square* and *Premium Times*. Many of them have been poached by hundreds of blogs and even the traditional media. It is my hope that the entrance they make into a book format in this volume will further consolidate their value as a store house of national memory. Each piece is a reflection on current affairs at the time it was written. Part of Nigeria's tragedy is the trap of the present. We live in the present. We are passionate about the present. We treat the past and the future as burdens, hence the absence of national memory and envisioning. If you remember events from our immediate past by reading this book, events long brushed under the carpet as we roll daily from present to present, my aim would have been partly achieved.

Part One:

Naija no dey Carry Last

President Umaru Yar'Adua's One Million Latrines

(March 2008)

Shame on the throng of unpatriotic pessimists and subversive elements who never reckon with the valiant efforts of Nigeria's leadership to "move the country forward" by taking the "dividends of democracy" to every doorstep in the country. From Abakaliki to Zungeru, "eminent elder statesmen", "respected chieftains", and "national stakeholders" in the PDP have joined hands with Justice James Ogebe and President Yar'Adua to ensure that the "national cake" is evenly sliced and devoured by every Nigerian. Yet, our career armchair critics continue to spew negative criticism while eating pizza and drinking hot chocolate in their comfortable Euro-American nest.

While some ungrateful Nigerians at home, slow to acknowledge the remarkable achievements of Mr. President, have mischievously christened him Baba Go-Slow, our unpatriotic critics abroad have exploited the enormous advantages of online dissemination at their disposal to megaphone that malicious alias. Shame on them! Allah has put them all to shame by granting Mr. President the unequalled wisdom to map out ways of ushering Nigerians into positive civilisation and positive modernity as opposed to the negative civilisation and negative modernity that have become a way of life in Euro-America and Asia.

In a story published in the March 19, 2008 edition of *ThisDay*, the Minister of (for?) Agriculture and Water Resources, Dr. Abba Ruma, was reported to have announced to Nigerians and the whole world that the federal government has concluded arrangements to construct one million latrines "within the next one year." Dr. Ruma made this announcement through a Permanent Secretary in his Ministry, Professor O. Afolabi, who represented him at an event organised to mark the World Water Day and to kick off World Sanitation Day. Yes, this brilliant initiative is so significant that only a combination of a Doctor and a Professor could have announced it. Let the critics know that this announcement was not made carelessly. After the President had his epiphany, commissions were set up to reflect on it; Nigerian and international experts were brought in to offer perspectives on the advantages of public latrines; legal opinion was provided by Nigeria's legal consultant in the United States. It was only after these painstaking efforts that Mr. President okayed the announcement.

Now, every Nigerian knows that one of the most shameful indices of our underdevelopment is the absence of public conveniences in our cities and villages. This has led to an endemic national culture of terrible hygiene. Everywhere, Nigerians do the small one and the big one in the open. Let's not talk about the sociology, politics, and tactics of open bowel movement in Lagos, or the individually creative strategies of disposal. Let's just talk about our 'Universities'. Over the years, our 'University' campuses have been particularly hard hit by this national disgrace. Imagine the sorry spectacle of boys and girls hitting the bush at night to "throw shot put" because of inadequate conveniences in their hostels. There have been reported cases of snakes aiming for dangling parts when male students stoop in the bush at night. Only God knows how many potential Nigerians will now never be born owing to the singular factor of snakes biting dangling parts when boys answer the call of nature in the bush. We have produced several generations of astute male and female shot putters in the last three decades. And who is not familiar with the sight of elderly women standing gingerly by the roadside and holding their *yeri* (skirt) to pee openly on their way to the farm or from the market?

It is in recognition of these sorry scenarios that Mr. President has decided to prioritise the construction of a whopping one million public latrines in one year as a key aspect of our millennium development goals. This is even more urgent than the provision of electricity. In one year, Mr. President will solve a problem that none of his predecessors has been imaginative enough to resolve. One million latrines! This is vision. This is foresight. This is bowel moving the nation forward. When next *Andrewed* and unpatriotic noisemakers like Okey Ndibe, Omoyele Sowore, Ogaga Ifowodo, Moses Ochonu, Obi Nwakanma, and Rudolf Okonkwo write crap about Mr. President being Baba Go-Slow, ask them if any President has ever thought of making it possible for their relatives at home to "ease themselves" (as we say in Naija) in privacy and with dignity. More importantly, which President has ever promised to do it in one year?

Mr. President deserves special commendation for having opted for the positive civilisation of latrines when he could very easily have fallen for the un-African and culturally insensitive lure of modern water-flushed toilets. The rush for negative civilisation is so alarming that in Japan, South Korea, China, and Euro-America, they are now opting for the retrogressive option of computerised public toilets that could be programmed to clean your behind when you're done doing your business. Is this not crazy? When will man learn to stop playing God? Not to be outdone, Ghana, Togo, Mali, Niger Republic, Burkina Faso, Cape Verde, Sao Tome and Principe, Lesotho, Swaziland, Benin Republic, and other insignificant African countries have now joined the madness of providing modern public conveniences for their people. How could these countries betray Africa in the 21st century? Have they never heard of Negritude? Did our ancestors use such corrupt instruments of modernity to move their bowels or empty their bladders? Hopefully, these African countries will retrace their steps and learn a thing or two from big brother Nigeria. Latrines are the African way to go.

It would be unfortunate if Mr. President stopped his government's admirable campaign against negative civilisation at the provision of latrines. We need a revolution. There are other areas of our national life yearning for precisely the kind of vision his government has shown with the latrines. There have been reports of a disturbing tendency by some commercial farmers in Nigeria to use retrogressive farm machines like tractors for large-scale food production. Apart from guzzling the scarce, polluted petrol that we import, this practice is also un-African. Mr. President should look into the possibility of importing one million hoes from China with immediate effect for distribution to our farmers at affordable prices. If the Chinese do not know what a hoe looks like, we can give them a sample. I strongly recommend the Agatu hoe. A policy of one man one hoe (apologies to T.M. Aluko) could provide jobs to one million graduates.

Speaking of oil importation, it is not uncommon for oil transporters to use modern oil tankers to ferry the imported product across the country. That is so wrong and Mr. President should correct this anomaly immediately. Every Nigerian knows that we have used a specialized tin container known as *garawa* or *gorodom* to transport liquid since 1914. Mr. President is surely aware that his northern kinsmen, who have been the most impoverished by the North's political stranglehold on federal power, have perfected the culture of commercial water distribution in *garawa*. Has Mr. President never seen the ubiquitous *mai ruwa*? He is all over Nigeria, selling water in two *garawa* slung across his shoulder with a stick. Why transport our imported petrol in tankers when we have the marvellous technology of the *mai ruwa*? Mr. President should immediately order the importation of one million *garawa* from China. We could distribute them to one million unemployed graduates. One million graduates with one million *garawa*, what better way to distribute fuel across Nigeria?

There is also this thing about the explosion of cell phones in Nigeria. Every Nigerian carries a minimum of three cell phones. This must be Senate President David Mark's worst nightmare. Imagine ordinary and poor Nigerians using models of cellphones that aren't even on sale yet in the United States. Mr. President, this is another evidence of negative modernisation. A corruption of our culture. Why should people who are only good enough for latrines in the 21st century be allowed to use Blackberries? Before you know it, Nigerians will start using iPhones. Can you imagine, Mr. President, an iPhone in a public latrine? Our ancestors communicated with drums and we should go back to our roots. It shouldn't be too hard to get the Chinese to make one million drums for us. The Yoruba gangan (talking drum) will be particularly effective for this patriotic national revolution in latrine-friendly, culturally-appropriate communication.

Finally, I have been to so many Nigerian embassies in Africa, Europe, and America. These diplomatic outposts are a disgrace to Mr. President's cultural revolution. They rent very modern buildings. Because they are chronically underfunded, they are frequently hounded by Shylock landlords for rent. In rare cases, Nigeria owns the buildings and there is no harassment. Why should our embassies be in modern buildings when our people will soon be blessed with one million latrines at home? Shouldn't our embassies be a reflection of who we are? Mr. President, may I humbly suggest that we construct thatched huts for all our embassies with immediate effect? We could start with preliminary huts in Washington, Ottawa, Tokyo, London, and Paris. Needless to say, this should not be limited to the chancery. Residential huts should also be constructed for our Ambassadors, who should consider wearing raffia skirts when presenting their letters of credence to the Presidents of their host countries. This, I'm afraid, is the only way that Nigeria's idea of progress and development in the 21st century can be taken seriously by the international community.

The Scramble for and Partition of Nigerian Ailments

(May 2008)

Very senior officials of the American, French, British and German governments recently held fruitful discussions with their Nigerian counterparts in Accra, Ghana. The purpose of the meeting was to amicably resolve disputes that have developed over exclusive rights to treat the ailments of Nigerian rulers and "top government functionaries." The summit was initially billed to take place in Abuja but Nigeria's representatives argued very vociferously that the timing clashed with their periodic official retreat in Accra, a city that has become their preferred location for carrying out the onerous task of governing the Nigerian people because it offers them a secure environment and stable power supply to do their work.

Convened by Nigeria's Federal Ministry of Health and the Health Committees in the Senate and the House of Representatives respectively, the meeting was attended by high-ranking officials from Aso Rock and top "chieftains" of the ruling People's Democratic Party. At issue was the need to map, territorialise, and establish treatment rights over the minor physical ailments of Nigerian rulers and senior government officials. This comes in recognition of the fact the minor ailments of Nigeria's leaders have become the second most valuable commodity to the four Western countries after Nigeria's oil. It will be recalled that France enjoyed a virtual monopoly over the treatment of Nigerian leaders in the 1980s after the tyrant, Ibrahim Babangida, went to Paris to treat radiculopathy. With France thus anointed by the dictator, Nigerian government officials, who until then were in the habit of treating their headaches and toothaches in London and New York, had to display their patriotism and loyalty to Babangida and Nigeria by shifting their medical safaris to France. This, obviously, did not go down well with the British and the Americans whose economies were severely affected. Thus commenced a prolonged underground "war" between these countries.

President Obasanjo prevented the situation from boiling over irredeemably when he assumed office in 1999. He achieved some sort of détente during his first term in office. Since he spent the entire four years ruling Nigeria from the skies, visiting every country that had an airport and, in some cases, offering to build airports for countries that had none in order to be able to visit them, there was no need for him to seek medical treatment in any of the feuding countries. An agreement was reached that allowed each of the Western countries in contention to station a permanent team of medical officials in the Nigerian presidential jet. This fragile peace was however shattered during Obasanjo's second term in office. A state governor, Diepreye Alamieyesiegha, needed to reduce the number one consequence of the incurable bacchanalia associated with government officials in Nigeria: the pot belly. Alamsco, as he is popularly called, headed to Germany for a tummy tuck. Hardly had the French Ambassador to Nigeria finished protesting this serious breach of the terms of the détente when Obasanjo's Vice President, Atiku Abubakar, had a minor knee dislocation while working out on the treadmill and rushed to London and Washington for treatment.

Unfortunately, Obasanjo was involved in a battle to determine who was less corrupt between him and Abubakar and was also stockpiling arms and ammunition in preparation for the do-or-die elections that would see the PDP capture Aso Rock for his anointed successor. He was therefore not in a situation to properly address the grievances of the French government over the disturbing actions of Alamsco and Atiku Abubakar.

Enter President Yar'Adua, the chief culprit in the situation that led to the Accra meeting! Without any consideration for the feelings of the Americans, the British, and the French, President Yar'Adua has been strolling to Germany every other week for medical treatment. Nigerians, cynical as ever, have been overheard saying that a branch of Aso Rock may soon open in Wiesbaden, Germany. President Yar'Adua has treated everything from cough to eczema, toothache to backache, and hand ache to leg ache in Germany. The Americans, the British, and the French are especially infuriated by the fact that the Nigerian government has so far offered no rational explanation as to why the extremely lucrative market in the treatment of presidential ailments should become the monopoly of the Germans. They fear that every Nigerian minister and state governor may now have to display loyalty to the President by shopping for doctors and hospitals in Germany.

Fortunately, the Accra meeting scored some positive points after protracted negotiations. An amicable agreement was reached. The anatomy of the Nigerian government official was mapped and territorially apportioned to each country present. It was decided that the head would go to the Germans. All ailments associated with the head of any Nigerian government official, or any Big Man with connections in the corridors of power, are henceforth to be treated exclusively in Germany. This includes popular ailments like headache, toothache, ear infection, sore throat, runny nose, and eye problems. The French got the torso, much to the displeasure of the Spanish delegation that was there only in an observer capacity. Henceforth, all ailments relating to the torso—chest pain, bellyache, and backache—are to be treated in France. The British got the hands and the legs and were careful to insist that this is not limited to serious injuries like fractures and dislocations. It also includes routine manicure and pedicure. The Americans agreed to give up all claims to any part of the anatomy of Nigerian government officials in exchange for exclusive rights over all cosmetic surgery needs of their wives. Henceforth, the wives of Nigerian government officials must go to California for their tummy tucks, face lift, liposuction, breast enlargement/reduction/lifting, nose jobs, skin toning and/or bleaching, etc.

A Memorandum of Understanding was presented and signed by all participants. The Nigerian delegation promised to deliver it expeditiously to the Presidency where it would be drafted into a binding treaty and sent to the National Assembly for prompt ratification. At the end of deliberations, the head of the German delegation gave a moving closing speech. History, he affirmed, has been made in Accra. He went down memory lane and recalled that the last time a meeting was held to share African property amicably among Western powers, it was all about land and resources. He remarked proudly that his country had had the extraordinary privilege of convening and hosting the said meeting in Berlin. Now, more than a hundred years later, it is the anatomy of the rulers of Africa's most populous nation that has been carved out among Western powers. The move from land and raw materials to human anatomy, he contended, is an indication of how brotherly and intimate the partnership between Africa and the West has become. He particularly stressed the point that Africans were not invited to the first meeting in Berlin. Now, not only were Africans present at this new partitioning, they convened and sponsored the meeting, in Accra, the spiritual home of African nationalism and independence. He concluded by telling the Nigerian delegation that they had every reason to be proud of themselves and hoped that the Nigerian people would learn to appreciate such a crop of dedicated and visionary leaders. In his speech, the leader of the British delegation apologised to the Germans for the arrest of Alamsco. The Germans had always claimed that Alamsco's arrest was an act of sabotage by the British, pure *bad belle* on the part of the British who merely wanted to "spoil market" for the Germans because Alamsco had his tummy tuck in Germany and not in Britain.

In his vote of thanks, the head of the Nigerian delegation thanked the Western powers for the selflessness with which they place the excellent medical facilities in their countries at the disposal of Nigerian leaders. What further proof of their commitment to the progress of Nigeria could there be? For it is only when Nigerian leaders enjoy good health that they are able to serve the people and deliver the dividends of democracy. By continuously treating the ailments of Nigeria's leaders, these Western countries have shown that they are committed to moving Nigeria forward and the Nigerian people would remain eternally grateful to them.

Breaking News: Nigeria Revolutionises the Discipline of Physics

(May 2008)

A high-powered delegation from the International Union of Pure and Applied Physics (IUPA), as well as representatives of the Nobel Prize Committee for Physics, has arrived in Abuja, Nigeria, on a fact-finding mission. The two important delegations aim to verify and authenticate the scientific essence of certain developments in Nigeria that have literally caused a tsunami in the global scientific community. If the mission ends on a positive note and things are authenticated, experts have surmised that Nigeria could reap tremendous benefits by becoming the Mecca of the world's most famous physicists. Some have even rumoured that Stephen Hawkins, the world's number one physicist, is merely waiting for the outcome of this mission to apply for Nigerian citizenship.

The importance of this epochal mission is underscored by the fact that the entire machinery of the Federal Government was mobilised to welcome the two visiting teams at a colourful airport ceremony. President Yar'Adua, members of his cabinet, all senior staff of Aso Rock, members of the National Assembly, PDP chieftains, and all state governors were present. Also present at the airport reception were eminent national stakeholders and dignitaries such as former President Olusegun Obasanjo, General Ibrahim Babangida, Alhaji Lamidi Adedibu, Chief Olabode George, Chief Chris Uba, Chief Dr.

Andy Uba, Chief Tony Anenih, Chief James Ibori, Chief Dr. Peter Odili, Chief Dr. Orji Uzor Kalu, Chief Lucky Igbinedion, and Almost-Ambassador Ahmadu Ali.

Can matter disappear? Can things just vaporise into a Black Hole that exists somewhere in Space? Can objects just vanish from our universe into ether? If the answer to any or all of these questions is yes, what happens to the law that matter or energy cannot be destroyed? These are questions that have exercised the minds of the world's best scientists, especially physicists, from Galileo to Newton, from Einstein to Hawkins. Although a new generation physicist like Ulf Leonhardt has pushed science to new limits by creating black holes, levitating objects or making things look like they disappeared, no physicist has ever had the last word—with evidence—on things disappearing without some sort of trace. Even the entire black hole theory does not come without claims of radiation and particles subsisting – trace! Something is always left. Atoms and molecules don't just vanish absolutely. Worst case scenario: they become something else if broken down beyond the limit of their endurance.

In essence, the closest thing to a disciplinary consensus is that matter does not just vanish absolutely without any trace atom or molecule existing somehow in some other form. This quasi-consensus was respected like a Papal Bull in the scientific community until 2004 when word filtered out that something was going on in Nigeria that could change the face of physics forever. An oil vessel, MT African Pride, was arrested for oil bunkering. The tanker was full of siphoned crude oil that was going to be shipped illegally out of Nigeria. It vanished in broad daylight into ether. A whole oil tanker and its entire cargo. No, it didn't sink. It didn't hit an iceberg. It just vanished in the hands of Nigerian officials. Into ether. No atoms or molecules left. No Hawkinsian radiation. No trace.

This curious development was sufficient to warrant a major inquiry by the IUPA and the Nobel Committee for Physics but some eminent scientists weighed in on the side of extreme circumspection. Professor James Watson was particularly vociferous in pouring cold water on any idea that such scientific developments could come out of Africa. You do not jettison centuries of scientific orthodoxy just because of one incident. If a revolution in science was going to take place, if some of the oldest laws of physics were going to change, you wanted to be able to announce to the world that the scientific breakthrough happened in Harvard, Yale, Oxford, Cambridge or the Sorbonne. How do you credit Africans with such a wonderful breakthrough? How do you credit Africans with making matter vanish into ether? And Nigerians for that matter!

The initial excitement eventually petered out until the world woke up recently to another Nigerian scientific first. This time, a plane ferrying several kilos of American dollars vanished into the black hole. It was a private plane bought with stolen money by a former governor. Since, like Houphouet Boigny, he also stole hundreds of kilos of American dollars—raw cash—from his state, he needed to transport the money out of the country. What better way than to transform his plane into a cargo plane and arrange for it to disappear with cargo and crew! It took off all right. It never landed. It never crashed. It just vaporised into the black hole. So significant is this development that when Willie Walsh, the CEO of British Airways, heard that Nigerians had disappeared an entire plane with cargo and crew, he secretly thanked his stars that his company's race-based profiling policy had provoked Nigerians into a mass boycott of the airline. Good riddance to bad rubbish, he thought. He couldn't put it beyond Nigerians to disappear one of his jumbo jets if the conditions were right. He now had proof. "Thank God they are staying away," he concluded in a secret memo to his staff.

The global scientific community, however, could no longer pretend that what was happening in Nigeria was a fluke. They agreed it was time to investigate what was possibly the greatest scientific scoop since the laws of gravity were discovered. A ship and a plane vaporising into the black hole with neither trace nor radiation? Now, this was a big one. They were still scrambling to put a committee together when Nigeria offered another landmark. This time, it was the mother of all scientific achievements. A whole senator of the Federal Republic vanished into ether. No atom or molecule left. Nothing. Stephen Hawkins released a statement. The Nobel organisation was contacted. The IUPA sprang into action. Within twenty-four hours, the delegations arrived Abuja.

In his speech at the airport reception, a proud President Yar'Adua attributed the spectacular scientific breakthroughs to his administration's determination to respect the Rule of Law in all things and at all times. In a gesture of respect for his predecessor, President Yar'Adua invited former President Obasanjo to address the visitors. An elated President Obasanjo noted that his administration played a key role by laying the foundation of these memorable developments. After all, the oil tanker vanished under his watch. What is more, he also donated his daughter, Senator Iyabo Obasanjo, as a guinea pig to the Integrated National Project for the Disappearance of Human and Material Evidence of Corruption, a new Federal agency created by the Yar'Adua administration. On hearing this, Babangida, Adedibu, Bode George, Chris Uba, Andy Uba, Tony Anenih, James Ibori, Peter Odili, Orji Uzor Kalu and Lucky Igbinedion interrupted the former President with a thunderous applause. President Obasanjo concluded by expressing optimism that the complex housing the Nigerian National Petroleum Corporation (NNPC) would also vanish into ether. "We have disappeared a ship, a plane, and a human being. These achievements will not be complete until we prove to our esteemed visitors and the whole world that we also have the science to disappear buildings, starting with the NNPC building. I suggest that we disappear the building quickly and save the monumental cost and distraction that a probe into the activities of the NNPC in the last eight years would present," Obasanjo enthused.

In a related development, ignorant and unpatriotic Nigerians have already begun to spread rumours that the CIA has infiltrated the two teams. The rumour mongers claim that the Americans are running a top secret espionage operation to steal the secrets of Nigeria's unbelievable scientific breakthrough. Although the CIA has a healthy record of disappearing people and things in parts of the Third World that are hostile to the capitalist appetite of Empire, they have never disappeared anything without a trace. There is always a trace and all it takes to ruin things for the CIA is a nosey journalist or an idle Congressman. That is why President Bush secretly declared the Nigerian breakthrough an asset of vital importance to the national security of the USA. If Nigeria has used her new and exclusive scientific knowledge to disappear a ship, a plane, and a woman without a trace, the Americans, it is claimed, are hoping to secretly apply that technique to Iran, Syria, Cuba, North Korea, and Venezuela. These countries have been behaving like impertinent mosquitoes on America's scrotum. When a mosquito perches on your scrotum and proceeds to feed on your blood from that inauspicious location, it is a bad idea to slap, kick, smash, or crush it. What you need to take care of the embarrassing situation is knowledge, the sort of scientific knowledge the Nigerians mysteriously stumbled upon! If the CIA succeeds in stealing Nigeria's most famous contribution to Physics, Iran, Syria, Cuba, North Korea and Venezuela could be made to vanish quietly into a Black Hole without a trace and the blame placed on Nigeria. So goes the theory of idle rumourmongers on the streets of Lagos.

Breaking News: Envelope and Stamp Riots Spread in Nigeria

(June 2008)

Kalakuta International News Agency (KINA) has reported violent clashes between rioters and security forces in major cities and towns in Nigeria. Protests have also flared up in villages across the country. The spontaneous nature of these countrywide riots is reminiscent of the SAP riots that engulfed the country over a decade ago. Unlike the SAP riots, however, Nigerians are not protesting the economic and infrastructural stasis that has ensured that the average Nigerian now enjoys a quality of life slightly lower than the lives of domestic dogs and cats in Euro-America; they are not protesting the institutionalisation of darkness by the Federal government agency, Problem Has Changed Name (PHCN); they are not protesting the conditions that have led to the emergence of a hefty chunk of Nigerian economic refugees in places like Darfur, Cotonou, N'Djamena, Conakry, Timbuktu, Ouagadougou, Gaborone, Freetown, Monrovia, Mogadishu, Kabul, Baghdad, Rangoon, and Kathmandu. No, they are not protesting these vistas of normalcy in Nigeria.

Unconfirmed reports attribute the riots to the sudden scarcity of postal envelopes and stamps in the country. When a people have acquired a benumbing reputation for an endless capacity to rationalise, explain away, and adapt to every misery under the sun; when they are known to shrug away every quotidian tragedy authored by the buffoons who govern them; when they are known to possess an endless supply of fatalistic phrases such as "*God dey*", "*ko* bad", "*we dey manage*", "*e go better*", "*how for do?*", "*man no die man no rotten*", it is usually the least expected and the most unusual stimulus that makes them snap. Of all the things that could cause a revolution, it had to be scarcity of bread in France! The French peasants couldn't find or afford their beloved baguette and they snapped in 1789! In Nigeria, people who have shrugged away horrible conditions of daily life since the tragedy authored by Lord Lugard in 1914 have now snapped because of the scarcity of stamps and envelopes! Something eventually makes even the most resilient people snap! The postal sector has ground to a halt in Nigeria as stamps and envelopes have mysteriously disappeared. NIPOST officials have gone underground, leaving room for wild speculations. Molue bus parliamentarians insist that only Chief James Ibori, the former governor of Delta state, has the capacity to make things disappear without a trace. If envelopes and stamps have vanished from Nigeria, President Yar'Adua must have secretly appointed Ibori, his bosom friend, as the Director-General of NIPOST.

This Molue parliament explanation was widely believed by Nigerians until some unpatriotic and disgruntled officials of the Federal Ministry of Justice leaked information to journalists that Chief Michael Aondoakaa, the nation's Attorney General and Minister of Justice, is the culprit responsible for the strange disappearance of envelopes and stamps. The disgruntled employees claimed that their boss has used up the entire domestic supply of stamps and envelopes. These employees reported that one of the first things he did on assumption of office was to add an extra designation to his office: Attorney General, Minister of Justice, and Stenographer-General of the Federal Republic of Nigeria. They claimed that Mr. Aondoakaa sometimes comes to the office dressed like the old colonial letter writers of yore.

Unfortunately for Nigeria, Mr. Aondoakaa is reported to take his duties as national letter writer much more seriously than his constitutional duties. Reports indicate that he has written letters to his counterparts in places like Britain, South Africa, Switzerland, France,

Belgium, Germany, Spain, Portugal, Italy, Luxemburg, the United States, Canada, Australia, New Zealand, Saudi Arabia, the United Arab Emirates, Kuwait, and so on and so forth. These are all popular destinations of Nigerian treasury looters, mostly former governors, ministers, and top government officials. Ever since post-September 11 realities forced these corrupt and greedy receivers of stolen Nigerian money to crack down on suspicious movement of funds in their banks, they have turned the heat on their former friends, Nigerian treasury looters. This has led to a rash of arrests of Nigerian officials in these countries. One jumped bail using African juju to outsmart the London Metropolitan Police and casually resumed office as a state governor in Nigeria, even with an international warrant of arrest out for him; another escaped the dragnet of the London Metropolitan Police dressed like a woman. A former Nigerian Vice President, furious that the FBI is sniffing too close for comfort, decided to sell his mansion in Potomac, Maryland and move to Dubai. There has also been a deluge of indictments of Nigerian government officials by these foreign countries on charges of money laundering, looting, forgery, 419, and behaviour unbecoming of public officers.

It is to stem the tide of these ugly developments that Mr. Aondoakaa embarked on the patriotic mission of transforming himself into Nigeria's Postmaster General. He considered this task all the more urgent given the fact that some of the treasury looters indicted by foreign governments in recent times are President Yar'Adua's friends and sponsors and are considered sacred cows by the Federal Government. Some of them have complimentary bedrooms in Aso Rock. Mr. Aondoakaa has thus spent most of his time in office writing letters of exculpation to any foreign government that has ever indicted a corrupt Nigerian government official. Sometimes, he writes attestations of integrity and good behaviour for these friends of President Yar'Adua. At other times, he writes letters expressing the Federal Government's opposition to the indictment of these criminals by overzealous foreign governments. Given Nigeria's prodigious production of treasury looters, Mr. Aondoakaa has had to write tonnes of letters to foreign governments and this explains the rapidity with which he used up Nigeria's entire domestic stock of envelopes and stamps. It is said that the Federal Government has awarded an emergency contract to the South African company that printed our ballot papers to print stamps and envelopes for immediate importation.

Sources claim that Mr. Aondoakaa has been very proactive in his letter writing duties. They claim that he has borrowed a leaf from President George Bush by adopting the American leader's pre-emptive strike philosophy. To this end, he has already written anticipatory letters of exculpation to all foreign governments on behalf of the current crop of serving governors and ministers in case it is revealed at the end of their tenure that they shipped stolen raw cash to those countries. Part of Mr. Aondoakaa's pre-emptive strategy has also been to write anticipatory letters of exculpation to anticipated new destinations of Nigerian loot – as things get hotter in the West, Nigerian treasury looters are having to find new safe havens for their loot. Consequently, Mr. Aondoakaa has written anticipatory letters to such places as Lesotho, Eritrea, Azerbaijan, Tajikistan, Kyrgyzstan, Uzbekistan, Tibet, Macau, Papua New Guinea, and Greenland. He warned these countries that, should Nigerian government officials decide to stash stolen funds in their banks in the future, the Federal Government would not tolerate any talk of indictment and prosecution of its eminent citizens. Reports also indicate that Mr. Aondoakaa has held fruitful discussions with Chief Ojo Maduekwe, Nigeria's Foreign Affairs minister, with a view to extending the benefits of citizen diplomacy to treasury looters indicted by foreign governments.

Meanwhile, President Yar'Adua has condemned the violent riots and vowed to deal ruthlessly with the rioters. Speaking through his spokesman, Mr. Segun Adeniyi, President Yar'Adua expressed confidence in his Attorney-General and commended him for ensuring that the letters of exculpation for anointed criminals in whom he is well pleased are written within the ambit of the Rule of Law.

President Obama's 2nd-Day Anniversary

(January 2009)

Americans can be exasperating. They just don't know how to do things. Professor Maurice Iwu was right. Americans have a whole lot to learn from Nigerians. Their inability to do things the proper way cost me a lot of money on January 23, 2009. President Obama had been sworn in three days earlier. He had said he was going to hit the ground running and he did. He attended ten balls on inauguration night, returned to the White House at almost midnight, and still had a Champagne nightcap with Oprah Winfrey and a handful of close friends.

The following day, his government was in full throttle. Even here in Ottawa, some three hundred kilometres away, I could feel the vibrations of governance. He attended a plethora of meetings to set the tone of his government, signed a welter of executive orders, and swore in officials who were instructed to get kicking immediately like the new boss. Day two was even more intense. More meetings in the White House, more articulations of policies and agendas, more executive orders, especially the order to close down Guantanamo Bay. Then there was the hugely symbolic working visit to Hillary Clinton's new lair at the State Department. By going there before the customary visit to the Pentagon, President Obama was giving the world an unmistakable signal: American diplomacy is back! Bye-bye to cowboy shock and awe!

After the State Department, it was back at the White House for more of the American people's work. I noticed that emphasis was on the things that could immediately have an impact on the life of the American Regular Joe. Governance must be felt immediately by the people. Then I had an epiphany while watching Anderson Cooper flirt as usual with Erica Hill towards the end of AC 360. Me I don't know for those two *sef.* Anyway, I digress. So I had an epiphany: By the end of his second day in office, President Obama had done considerable more governing than Alhaji Umar Yar'Adua who is approaching his third year in Nigeria! All the Nigerian president has been able to do in two years is to cobble together two successively sleepy cabinets.

Somebody does more governing in two days than the Nigerian President has done in two years? Surely, Americans know what to do. So, on day three, I rushed to the nearest newspaper store and bought major American newspapers: *USA TODAY*, *New York Times*, *Washington Post*, and *Wall Street Journal.* I eagerly flipped to the centre spread of each paper. Nothing! What? Are these Americans kidding me? No paid centre spread ads congratulating President Obama on the 2nd day anniversary of his spectacular Presidency? Are there no State Governors in America? No Federal Ministers – sorry, Secretaries? No Local Government Chairmen – sorry, Mayors? No Stakeholders? No Party Chieftains? Well, since Americans won't do it, someone's gotta do it. So, I took it upon my patriotic self to draft a paid ad, just to give President Obama a taste of what he would have seen in national newspapers had Americans done things the Nigerian way. Here is what my centrespread ad in *New York Times* looks like:

Hurray! Hurray!! Hurray!!!
Three Hearty Cheers to a Born Achiever: His Excellency Barrister Barack Hussein Obama, the Executive President of the United States of America, Grand Commander of the Order of the Potomac (GCOP).

Dear President Obama, on behalf of myself, my loving wives, my children, and the people of the State of New Jersey, accept our heartfelt celebration of your phenomenal achievements on this wonderful 2nd-day anniversary of your assumption of office. Your exemplary leadership and outstanding achievements in *the last two days are indeed a confirmation of the nationally-held view that you have been divinely anointed to steer the ship of state and move the US forward at this crucial stage of our national life. By the same token, we respectfully extend our greetings and fellowship to our loving mother of the nation, Her Excellency Barrister Mrs. Michelle Obama, for the successful launching of her pet project, The Rural Woman Rocks! I hereby announce a token donation of three million dollars to Her Excellency's project on behalf of the State of New Jersey with immediate effect. We look forward to your first familiarisation tour of our beautiful state.*

Long live Your Excellency!
Long live the State of New Jersey!!
Long live the United States of America!!!
HIP HIP HIP, HURRAY!
Signed:
His Excellency Architect Dr XYZ
The Executive Governor, State of New Jersey.

NAFDAC-Certified Virgins

(February 2009)

Pliny the Elder gave his folks in Ancient Rome one of the most famous sayings about Africa: *ex Africa semper aliquid novi* (from Africa always something new)! The Romans were in too much of a hurry. They spoke several centuries too early. They should have waited until 1914 for the birth of Chief Obafemi Awolowo's "mere geographical expression." They would have been able to declare: *ex Nigeria semper aliquid novi*. There is just never a dull moment in good old Naija. Never a lull in our endless supply of farce and that is precisely what makes Nigeria tick. Last week, we entertained the world by unveiling the first goat ever to be arrested for armed robbery in the history of humanity, sorry, I meant to say history of caprinity.

We have followed up on this remarkable feat by giving the world what US-based Nigerian scholar, Valentine Ojo, would call an unbeatable "weekend relaxation treat." We have now invented the world's most effective formula for conflict resolution, courtesy of Ambassador Segun Olusola's African Refugee Foundation. Here's *Daily Champion* of Friday January 30, 2009 on the latest first from Nigeria: "FOUNDER of the African Refugee Foundation (ARF), Ambassador Olusegun Olusola, last weekend conferred the Agents of Peace of ARF on 41 winners of female virginity contest. He said that the award was his own way of celebrating the 41 virgins, who participated in the 2nd Nigerian Virgin Girls Celebration organised last year by Princess Adediran Adunni in Lagos. *Amb. Olusola said the awardees whose ages ranged from 15 and above, have demonstrated that they can be trusted in resolving conflicts as volunteers of the ARF* (my emphasis). While encouraging the girls to remain chaste as long as necessary, the ARF boss advised young people especially girls to live a pious life that would be useful to them and their community. Meanwhile, the 41 virgins would also enjoy free gynaecological care if they remained chastise (sic)."

I had to read the report several times to make sure that the bone-chilling freezing temperature of Ottawa wasn't doing funny things to my brain. Then I saw the same news report in other newspapers. Teenage girls as young as fifteen are becoming certified crisis managers and agents of peace in Nigeria? Just by keeping their hymens unruffled? Well, I have some suggestions on how these national assets could be deployed for optimal results. President Barack Obama has just appointed Mr. George Mitchell as his Special Envoy to the Middle East. In fact, Mr. Mitchell left for the region only last week to try and broker a peace agreement between Israelis and Palestinians. Mr. Mitchell should be fired immediately. The Nigerian Ambassador to the United States should seek an emergency audience with President Obama and tell him that Nigeria now has an African solution to the intractable Israeli-Palestinian conflict. Five of our newly-minted virgin conflict managers should be deployed in the Middle East as President Obama's Peace Envoys. We are left with thirty-six. Charity begins at home. We must send a virgin to each of the thirty-six conflict-prone states of the Federation. Subsequent batches of certified virgins should be deployed in Darfur, Zimbabwe, Somalia and Congo.

We must prepare for potential drawbacks. We have been producing too many virgins in Nigeria lately. Perhaps we are manufacturing virgins out of some desperate desire to have something that works in Nigeria? If we can't have sustainable democracy, if we can't have sustainable development, we can at least have sustainable hymenization. First, Covenant University insisted on subjecting all her female undergraduate students to virginity tests until the Nigerian Universities Commission, pushed by public outrage, called the Christian *Ayatollah* owners of that University to order. Now, African Refugee Foundation has dabbled into the business of manufacturing pubescent virgins. My fear is that Nigeria may become the destination of the ghost of every ambitious suicide bomber who blows himself up in the Middle East in anticipation of the reward of seventy-six virgins in paradise. Why blow yourself up and travel all the way to paradise when your ghost can just migrate to Nigeria and be rewarded here on earth with the NAFDAC-certified virgins we are producing left, right, and centre? Forget *Al-Janna*. The reward of martyrdom is now in Lagos. I won't be surprised if we start reading reports about sightings of Arab-looking ghosts and apparitions in Nigeria.

A feminist backlash is inevitable. I can picture the angry faces of some of my feminist sisters in Africanist scholarship when they read about this latest assault on womanhood by a Nigerian patriarchy clever enough to instrumentalise a woman, Princess Adediran Adunni, who organised the virginity pageant on behalf of men. African Refugee Foundation should brace itself up for the coming storm. The only way to prevent this is for the Foundation to ensure gender equity by subjecting pubescent boys to virginity tests and making them Peace Envoys if they pass the test. If we can turn a human being into a goat and arrest it for armed robbery, it shouldn't be too difficult for us to devise scientific ways of determining if a teenage boy has eaten bearded meat or not, *abi*?

Confirmation Hearing 101 for Senator David Mark & Co

(February 2009)

I am disappointed that Senate President, David Mark, did not lead a delegation of Nigerian Senators to Washington to observe the recent Senate confirmation hearings for Barack Obama's cabinet nominees. In fact, had Nigeria's entire Senate moved to Washington during this process, no Nigerian would have dismissed the trip as an estacode-guzzling proposition. Our polity is in dire need of what our distinguished senators could have learnt from such a classroom experience in the US Capitol. I know a few Nigerians in Washington who, desperate for change at home, would have supplied notepads, jotters, and pens to the apprentice senators as their contribution to national development. If necessary, I would have shipped chalk and wooden black slates to them to facilitate their classroom experience in Washington.

Had Senator David Mark and his fellow lawmakers registered for and attended the Confirmation Hearing 101 course in Washington, they would have learnt crucial lessons that would have reduced their lamentable ignorance of confirmation procedures and saved the Nigerian people the agony of witnessing the periodic circus they call senate confirmation hearings in Abuja. For starters, Senator Mark and co would have witnessed the rigorous grilling of as important a figure as Hillary Rodham Clinton by her former senate colleagues. They would have been surprised—no, shocked— that the John Kerry-led Foreign Relations Committee didn't just ask this famous American and former First Lady to "take a bow" and be sworn into office three seconds later.

Imagine Hillary Clinton's Nigerian equivalent, Maryam Babangida, appearing for confirmation before David Mark and his people in Abuja! We would have had a bunch of cackling sycophants over-reaching themselves to play footsie with her ego: "Ah, Madam, welcome to your Senate confirmation hearing, ma. Hope Her Excellency had a nice trip to Abuja *o*? What about our General, ma? What, he accompanied you to Abuja *ke*? He really shouldn't have bothered, ma. We are his boys. Who are we to invite an elder statesman? Take a bow, ma. Winner ooo winner, winner ooo winner, Her Excellency *you don win o* winner *pata pata you go win* forever winner. Bye-bye, ma."

Back in Washington, our senators would have witnessed the gruelling questioning of such power brokers as Timothy Geithner, Eric Holder and Tom Daschle. They would have been dumbfounded that Senator Daschle's nomination as Obama's Health and Human Services Secretary collapsed under the weight of the sin of tax evasion. In their Abuja universe, it would be unthinkable to have a former Senate President appear for confirmation for a cabinet position and suffer the indignity of even being questioned about his taxes in the first place! The Nigerian equivalents of the Obama nominees whose candidacies fell through are all "big men", "stakeholders", and "chieftains" who, by definition, are above the laws of the land and such demeaning processes as confirmation hearings, hence the perfunctory ritual of taking a bow.

The Nigerian people pay a considerable price for this tragic culture of demission on the part of our Senators. Their comical approach to confirmation hearings largely explains how President Yar'Adua has been able to get away with two of the most somnambulistic cabinets in the nation's history. It also explains the new meaning we have given to multitasking in Nigeria. It is possible for a single individual with a Bachelor's degree in Islamic and Arabic studies, who has served in every administration since Lord Lugard, to survive three cabinet reshuffles in the life of a single administration, moving from, say, the

Ministry of Finance to the Ministry of Information and, finally, to the Ministry of Science and Technology. Naturally, this individual would face three separate senate confirmation hearings, claiming expertise in all these areas and taking the perfunctory bow each time.

There is one important last lesson our senators could have learnt in Washington: the proper way to use legislative aides and personal assistants. They would have noticed that each confirmation hearing committee member was in session with his or her aides seated behind him or her. They would have noticed the endless passing of scribbled notes between each senator and his/her aides. These are the aides who would have spent thousands of hours poring over documents, verifying the resume of the Cabinet nominee, checking and cross-checking every detail, and preparing the interventions of their principals. In Abuja, the counterparts of these congressional aides loiter in the corridors of the National Assembly, flashing important-looking business cards at every opportunity. Yet, all they really do is carry the briefcases and the cell phones of their principals, buy recharge cards, kola nuts, suya, and newspapers, and make themselves generally useful as part of the big man's "protocol."

Nigerianising Nigeria's Embassies

(February 2009)

Career badmouthers of Nigeria's Federal Government have gone gaga over the news that a modest sum of ₦1.5 billion has been earmarked in the 2009 budget "to fuel generators" in Nigeria's Embassies and Consulates abroad. Cynics, who have made up their minds never to give President Yar'Adua credit for anything, have gone to town, running their mouths over the proposition of making funds available for our missions to buy petrol and diesel for their stand-by generators in places like the United States, Canada, Britain, France, Germany, Belgium and South Africa. Unable to appreciate the brilliance of this initiative, the editors of *Daily Trust* leered in their edition of February 24, 2009: "*the Federal Government may have confused this country's epileptic power situation as the norm in other countries because ₦ 1.5 billion has been earmarked in the 2009 budget to fuel generators in this country's missions abroad.*"

Not to be outdone, diasporic Nigerians, especially the "internet warriors" among them, have taken typical Nigerian *bad belle* to the point of insinuating that not a single Embassy will receive the allocated funds. They aver that those who came up with the idea in Aso Rock to earmark generator fuel funds for Embassies located in countries where electricity does not blink are actually not as foolish as their proposal makes them out to be. These unpatriotic elements would have us believe that the ₦ 1.5 billion could end up taking a sabbatical in private bank accounts. And these are the most generous comments I've heard and read so far.

I beg to differ. President Yar'Adua is spot on with this budgetary provision. I don't see why he should be blamed for the ignorance of his detractors. The critics miss one crucial point. Diplomatic missions are considered sovereign territories of their respective countries. The moment I enter the Nigerian High Commision in Ottawa, I'm technically on Nigerian soil/territory. I'm not in Canada. If Nigerian Embassies abroad are technically on Nigerian soil, it stands to reason that those missions must mirror conditions in Nigeria. They must show how we are and who we are. Those missions *must be* Nigeria. Uninterrupted electricity is not Nigerian, hence the Federal Government's decision to begin the Nigerianisation process of our Embassies in that vital area. Besides, why should our Ambassadors be exposed to the dangers of regular electricity in their countries of accreditation while their bosses in the Foreign Affairs Ministry and Aso Rock run the affairs of the country on generators?

I have been to many Nigerian missions in Europe and the Americas, and I haven't found any of them sufficiently Nigerian. Consider our missions in the US and Britain, for example. Only their dysfunctional and hardly-ever-updated websites and service that sometimes replicates the atmosphere in a ministry or local government secretariat back home remind you that those missions are on Nigerian soil. Thus, the Federal Government must be commended for this Nigerianisation initiative that will certainly move our missions towards a more authentic Nigerian-ness. In order to ensure the smooth sail of this excellent initiative, I want to make the following suggestions to President Yar'Adua. Giving our Embassies money to buy petrol for their generators is only a start. We must build on that solid foundation by instructing all our Ambassadors to purchase Mikano generators for their missions immediately. None of our missions in Euro-America currently has a generator, and that is a shame. I hope provisions are also made in the budget for our Embassies to buy drums and jerry cans for storing their petrol.

Once the generators are in place, the Federal government must contact the relevant electricity company in each country and sign a bilateral agreement or a memorandum of understanding that would ensure epileptic power supply to our missions in order to have them operate in Nigerian conditions. For instance, Ottawa Hydro must be told that they have to “take light” at ourHigh Commision on Metcalfe Street every twenty minutes in order to create Nigerian conditions and an enabling environment for the use of the new generator that the mission must purchase without delay.

I have equally noticed that water runs from the tap in all our Embassies in Euro-America. I noticed this horrifyingly anti-Nigerian phenomenon the last time I was at our High Commision in Ottawa. I was rightfully dismayed and disgusted. May I suggest to President Yar’Adua that as soon as we are done with electricity and generators, we should move to have our Embassies disconnected from the public water grid in their host countries? This will create the Nigerian condition of dry taps making that *pooooooooooo* sound when you turn them on. We can then earmark money for the digging of boreholes in our Embassies in Euro-America and wells in our Embassies in Africa in the 2010 budget.

Other Nigerianising measures the President may want to consider in the future include: digging open sewage (gutter) around our Embassies in Euro-America starting with the major ones in London and Washington, erecting gates like we have in Nigeria in front of each Embassy and posting *maiguards* from home to man the gates. The *maiguards* must be instructed to sell retail stuff like sweet, cigarettes, biscuits, kola nuts, *alabukun* and recharge cards – all displayed on a tray at their duty post. Finally, we must dig respectable potholes on the stretch of road leading to our Embassies. This will involve intense negotiations with the host countries. If these suggestions are taken seriously and executed, President Yar’Adua would have given Nigerians abroad Embassies they can relate to. We’ll be eternally grateful.

The Prince of Peace

(June 2009)

No, I am not talking about the son of a Nazarene carpenter called Joseph. I am talking about Prince Olagunsoye Oyinlola, the Governor of Osun state, who now seems determined to outdo Mary's famous son in the peace department. It is beginning to look like "the dividends of democracy" for the people of Osun State lies in their ability to boast that the do-or-die selection methods of the PDP have transformed them into privileged recipients of a deputy Jesus Christ in the person of Olagunsoye Oyinlola, Nigeria's most prolific peacemaker.

First was the peace accord he brokered between former President Olusegun Obasanjo and his estranged former Vice President, Atiku Abubakar. Then the Prince of Peace was off to Minna for a peace treaty between General Ibrahim Babangida and his would-be nemesis, Major Saliba Mukoro, leader and mastermind of the April 22, 1990 Orkar coup. Off to Ibadan, where the Prince of Peace sealed yet another peace deal between Olusegun Obasanjo and former Oyo State governor, Senator Rashidi Ladoja.

As long as the people of Osun state are cool with it, there is nothing wrong with Prince Oyinlola rolling from state to state to gather the moss of peace treaties even as governance in his domain goes the way of everything the PDP touches – failure. What we, the Nigerian people, need to resist are the surreptitious registers of canonisation and the well-choreographed modes of aggrandisement that our emergency troubadours of peace are foisting on the national space of meaning. There is such a thing as speaking for a nation's past and her present. The catch always lies in who gets to speak for a nation's past and present. The people, or their traducers in the political elite.

Olagunsoye Oyinlola and his fellow jokers in the emergent Peace Industry are attempting to speak for our past and present in order to smuggle their rickety legacy into our future. If in doubt, examine their vocabulary. Oyinlola declared that kissing and making up by Obasanjo and Atiku was the best thing that ever happened to Nigeria. The occasion was "historic", "epochal", and deserving of every grandiose and delusional adjective that Oyinlola could fish from the dictionary. The reconciliation between Ibrahim Babangida and Major Mukoro was also described as "historic." Oyinlola even allowed himself some effusive extra mileage in hyperbole: the reconciliation of the coupists will allow Oyinlola to "move the country forward." The same canonising vocabulary was at work as our friends came out of the Ibadan peace meeting between Obasanjo, Rashidi Ladoja, Alao Akala, and the Prince of Peace.

There is nothing new in Oyinlola's adventures. Politicians constantly redraw the map of political alliances. Bruised egos deemed of continuous value to the perpetuation of group interest are soothed, old enemies fall into the bed of common interests, existing alliances are recalibrated even as new liaisons are formed towards winning elections (if you are in the civilised world) or capturing power (if you are in Nigeria). What is insufferable is the presumptuousness that has led Oyinlola to elevate moves calculated to earn him some national presence in furtherance of future ambitions, and to give a semblance of continuous relevance to the likes of Olusegun Obasanjo and Ibrahim Babangida, to the status of historic national moments.

The ease with which members of Nigeria's *lootocracy* equate their inconsequential shenanigans with our destiny is a clear indication of how low our stock has fallen as a people. Our rulers are perpetually insulting us. One minute Dimeji Bankole is canonising himself a leader; the next minute Oyinlola is decreeing what is historic. It is particularly annoying that Babangida's mini-Robespierran ego gets equated with our history and destiny at every opportunity. Two coupists meet to drink beer in Minna and that is a "historic" act that will "move Nigeria forward!" The only "historic" miss I see here is that Gideon Orkar, who remains a hero in my book, did not get Babangida.

There is no telling what next Oyinlola will declare historic. We are even getting dangerously close to a point where one of these charlatans ruling and ruining Nigeria will go to the toilet in the morning and declare that whatever he did therein to unburden his bowels is "historic", "epochal", and will "move Nigeria forward." Olagunsoye Oyinlola should be advised to concentrate on what his political ilk does best—looting, rigging, electoral violence— and leave the determination of what is historic to the Nigerian people.

Mrs. Clinton, Please Do Not Come to Nigeria!

(August 2009)

Dear Mrs. Hillary Clinton,

Good afternoon ma. I hope this letter meets you in good condition of health. If so, doxology. Apologies that I had to send the letter by DHL. I was going to email it but it occurred to me that an email written by a Nigerian living in Nigeria may not pass through the eye of the needle of the powerful Nigerian 419 email spam blocker now installed in all American government computers in accordance with the provisions of the 30th Amendment to the US Constitution otherwise known as the Nigerian Amendment. I also tried to send the letter to you through your Under-Secretary of State to Nigeria, Mr. Ojo Maduekwe, but was told that he was not planning one of his infrequent trips to Nigeria from his base in the US any time soon.

Madam Secretary Ma, it is with great dismay that I read in our newspapers that you will be visiting Abuja later this week in a 'make una no vex' attempt to placate our ogas here who are still sulking and smarting from losing President Obama to Ghana. It is being widely reported here that you are coming to "talk tough" about corruption and electoral malpractices. Madam Secretary Ma, ordinary Nigerians like me, all victims of the people who will host you in Abuja, have been having a belly laugh at our paraga and burukutu joints. You are coming to Abuja to preach against corruption and electoral malpractices? You remind us of the tortoise in the folktale who went to an assembly of cats to talk tough about the need for them to take rats off the menu.

That is not why I am writing and asking you to reconsider this trip *o*. That is just a small aside. Most Nigerians like me do not want you to come because we are the ones who will bear the brunt of the visit. Since you will not get to see any of us, it is difficult for one to explain to you how your visit will trample on our dignity and humanity. You see, when you host important dignitaries and world leaders in Washington, you always design the visits to have the most minimal disruption on the normal routine of the citizens of your country living in Washington. If your compatriots desire to be part of the action, you create a rope line where they can line up to see the modest motorcade and, depending on the circumstances, shake hands and have photo-ops with the visitor. Madam Secretary Ma, your hosts in Abuja believe that the human dignity of the Nigerian citizen stops where the two-kilometre-long motorcade of any foreign visitor begins. And because you are a visitor of timbre and calibre, forty-eight hours to your arrival, we would have been cleared off the streets, from within a forty mile radius of wherever you will be in Abuja. Roads will be closed and businesses disrupted. The clearing exercise is never funny, Ma. It is done by soldiers and anti-riot policemen with koboko, tear gas, machine guns, and tanks. They will kick the heck out of our butts to ensure that our offensive presence as Nigerians does not mar your trip.

If you think I am lying Ma, you will see those soldiers and anti-riot policemen throughout your visit. You will see tanks and so many other things you never see when receiving Presidents and world leaders in Washington. In fact, the presence of troops and tanks mobilised by our rulers to give you maximum security and keep us at bay will remind you of that little situation in Bosnia when you had to dodge sniper fire. As you must have been briefed by the Nigerian Desk at the African Desk at the State Department, we are the Giant of Africa and we do things giantly. So, we all live in giant darkness here because 140 million of us share a little under 2000 megawatts of electricity. We are targeting

6000 megawatts by 2015 in order to become one of the world's top 20 economies five years later Ma. Anyway Ma, we ration our roughly 2000 megawatts. What that means, Ma, is that each Nigerian is entitled to about 3 hours of electricity per month.

Now that you are coming Ma, your hosts in Abuja will have to divert every single megawatt meant for us to places like Aso Rock, the National Assembly, Transcorp Hilton Hotel (if you stay there). Normally they run all those places on generators imported from Japan and China but they may not want you to hear all that generator noise. And there is no telling if the petrol and diesel they import to run those generators are not adulterated. They can't run the risk of exposing you to the dangerous fumes reserved exclusively for Nigerian citizens. So, every megawatt we have in the country will be diverted for your exclusive use Ma. They may even have to borrow a few more megawatts from Benin Republic and Cameroon just to make sure that you enjoy uninterrupted electricity throughout your stay. Every second you enjoy electricity in Nigeria Ma, it is being taken away from one hundred thirty-nine million, nine hundred ninety-seven thousand people. I am leaving out the 3000 morons responsible for the situation, Ma, since it doesn't really affect them. They are your hosts and our rulers. Ma, knowing what you now know, would you want to deny Nigerians their right to 3 hours of electricity per month?

I don't know if you are spending one or two nights in Abuja but I must tell you that a visit like yours normally translates to a temporary suspension of governance in Nigeria. I can assure that since last week, nobody of consequence is "on seat" in Abuja and at the state capitals. They have stopped doing the business of the people to prepare "for our august visitor." Don't be surprised that Governors and "First Ladies" of far-flung states like Taraba and Lagos may have arrived Abuja over a week ago to be part of the action. Hundreds of "welcome committees" are already at work in every government building in Abuja, running "miscellaneous expenses" to welcome you. Ma, you can only imagine the millions of man hours we are going to lose to this visit.

There is also the damage to our treasury. Just wait until you hear how much your hosts will eventually claim they spent on entertainment and African hospitality during your visit. It could end up competing favourably with the entire monthly budget of the State Department. That brings me again to the matter of corruption, Ma. Well, you are not going to see corruption in Nigeria. It is invisible. But you are going to eat corruption. And drink corruption. You see, we may not be a democracy like certain countries in Africa but we are proud to run a fledgling *contractocracy*. That means that every grain of rice you will eat during your visit was awarded as a heavily over-inflated contract to somebody. Every slice of bread you will eat at breakfast is the product of an over-inflated contract. Every bottle of water you will drink was contracted out and invoiced beyond the going rate at the Waldorf Astoria. I will spare you the details of the roads travelled by those who got those contracts to supply food and drinks and how they said "thank you" to those who awarded the contracts at the Ministry.

There is one good news, Ma. If you do come, our National Assembly will have a full house while you are here. Our Distinguished Senators and Honourable Reps will all want a piece of the action. Normally Ma, they hardly ever come to work. They only come infrequently to collect *Ghana-must-go* and disappear. No, Ma, they are not going to Ghana. I said *Ghana-must-go*. *Em, em, em*, that is a bag, Ma. No, Ma, it is not used to store bills and house publications. Well, *em*, it stores bills but not the bills you have in mind. Anyway, Ma, should you reject my advice not to come, let me take it upon my humble self to offer you the following travel tips:

1. Travel with ear muffs. Your motorcade will be loudly sirened 24/7.
2. Leave the word "Mr." in Washington. You won't need it at any time in Abuja.
3. Check the memo that officials of the American Embassy in Abuja will give you as soon as you land. It will contain instructions on how, when, and where to use Chief, Alhaji, Dr., Your Excellency Sir, Your Excellency Ma and so on and so forth.

4. If a Governor comes to welcome you, do not call him Mr. Governor. It is "Your Excellency The Executive Governor." It is a worse offense not to address his wife as "Your Excellency The First Lady."
5. If you visit the National Assembly, every Senator is "Distinguished", and every Rep is Honourable. Learn to take a bow.
6. If, despite the diversion of every single megawatt in the country for your use, NEPA still strikes (see American Embassy memo for meaning of expression), make light conversation with your hosts as you wait for the generator to kick in. Smile and reassure them with sentences like "*Ah*, Chief, you know these things happen everywhere. No country is perfect."
7. Lest you feel crowded, apart from their retinue of aides, every member of the Executive or the Legislature you meet has four personal serfs otherwise known as Personal Assistants. Each of the first three carry one of the bosses' three cell phones and the fourth carries his briefcase or her handbag. (See Embassy memo for further details.)
8. If you bump into a man called Michael Aondoakaa, give him stamps and envelopes. He'll appreciate it. He loves to write letters (See the CIA's file on him for more details.)

If I have other suggestions, I will not hesitate to let you know, Ma. I trust that you will carefully consider everything I have written here.

Yours respectfully,
Ordinary Nigerian.

The PDP Memos on Archbishop John Olorunfemi Onaiyekan

(October 2009)

From: Aso Rock
To: PDP National Secretariat and Office of the Senate President
Subject: Archbishop John Olorunfemi Onaiyekan
Date: October 5, 2009
Code: Classified Top Secret/Circulate on Need to Know Basis

Gentlemen, the Presidency is worried by the spate of class suicide and elite back-stabbing that has seemingly engulfed the country. First, it was the Sultan of Sokoto addressing the public in Kaduna and telling them that nothing works in Nigeria. He claimed, feloniously and erroneously, that there is "no light, no water, no food, no security" in Nigeria. Now, the Catholic Archbishop of Abuja Archdiocese, John Olorunfemi Onaiyekan, has joined forces with the unpatriotic detractors of the current administration. Hear him talk about Nigeria in a recent media interview: "*Any nation that does not care about good governance builds itself on lies, does not care about the less privileged within its midst, the leaders are only interested in their own selfish interest and convenience and close their eyes completely to the poor, the sick, the aged and the youths and basic amenities are not their top priority, where roads are untended, factories are allowed to die, schools stay closed for months and nobody is worried, such a nation cannot say that they are building themselves into anything great. Such a nation is killing itself.*" He didn't stop at that: "*Do not steal from the poor people because every money you steal from the government, you are stealing from the poor.*" These unpatriotic statements, first from the Sultan and now from the Archbishop, are undoubtedly at variance with the spirit of the seven-point agenda. Consequently, Mr. President is of the opinion that our Great Party needs to do something urgently about Archbishop Onaiyekan in order to move the country forward and restore the rule of law.

Cc: Elder Chieftain Stakeholder James Ibori
Chief Michael Aondoakaa (SAN)
Chief Dr Andy Uba

From: PDP National Secretariat (Vincent Ogbulafor)
To: The Presidency and the Office of the Senate President
Subject: Archbishop John Olorunfemi Onaiyekan
Date: October 6, 2009
Code: Classified Top Secret/Circulate on Need to Know Basis

Acknowledging receipt of yours. The Party agrees with the President. All hands must be on the deck to stem the tide of unpatriotic statements and actions in high places. Talk like this could jeopardise our sixty-year rolling plan. Because he is a respected man of God, too many otherwise law-abiding and patriotic Nigerians may be tempted to believe Archbishop Onaiyekan. Counter-measures are therefore in order. Given his considerable expertise in the pacification of primitive and unpatriotic Nigerians abroad, may I humbly suggest that we delegate that responsibility to our venerated colleague and Distinguished President of the Senate of the Federal Republic?

Cc: Elder Chieftain Stakeholder James Ibori
Chief Michael Aondoakaa (SAN)
Chief Dr Andy Uba

From: The National Assembly (Office of the Senate President)
To: The Presidency and PDP National Secretariat
Subject: Archbishop John Olorunfemi Onaiyekan
Date: October 6, 2009
Code: Classified Top Secret/Circulate on Need to Know Basis

Acknowledging receipt of memos. This is a matter of urgent national importance. Thanks, Mr. Party Chairman, for acknowledging my expertise in identifying and dealing with unpatriotic Nigerians, especially those noisemakers abroad. My experience would definitely come in handy. What do the President and the Party have in mind? The Abacha solution or the Babangida solution?

Cc: Elder Chieftain Stakeholder James Ibori
Chief Michael Aondoakaa (SAN)
Chief Dr Andy Uba

From: Aso Rock
To: PDP National Secretariat and Office of the Senate President
Subject: Archbishop John Olorunfemi Onaiyekan
Date: October 5, 2009
Code: Classified Top Secret/Circulate on Need to Know Basis

Thanks, gentlemen, for your prompt responses and the seriousness with which you have taken this matter into consideration. To answer the question of the Senate President, the Abacha solution is tempting but very dangerous. Nobody will buy it even if we make it look like an accident. Besides, we risk a major international incident with the Vatican and an international community that is already so unpatriotic and anti-Nigeria. That is why we have imposed sanctions on the international community by not attending G20 meetings and the UN General Assembly. And then, there is the habitual bad faith of the Nigerian people. They will read meaning into the fact that the Sultan said pretty much the same thing and did not get the Abacha treatment. They would read tribalism and northern privilege into the whole thing. In the circumstances, Mr. President is in favour of the Babangida solution.

Cc: Elder Chieftain Stakeholder James Ibori
Chief Michael Aondoakaa (SAN)
Chief Dr Andy Uba

From: PDP National Secretariat (Vincent Ogbulafor)
To: The Presidency and the Office of the Senate President
Subject: Archbishop John Olorunfemi Onaiyekan
Date: October 6, 2009
Code: Classified Top Secret/Circulate on Need to Know Basis

I must again agree with and admire the President's considerable wisdom. The Abacha solution is indeed tempting but we cannot afford it. That loud-mouthed Professor with the famous white mane will go about town calling us a nest of killers all over again. I support the Babangida method. A point of correction though: Archbishop John Olorunfemi Onaiyekan is a northerner like the Sultan. He is from Kabba in Kogi state. That makes him a technical Hausa man like our respected party elder from Mopa in Kogi state, the late Chief Sunday Bolorunduro Awoniyi.

Cc: Elder Chieftain Stakeholder James Ibori
Chief Michael Aondoakaa (SAN)
Chief Dr Andy Uba

From: The National Assembly (Office of the Senate President)
To: The Presidency and PDP National Secretariat
Subject: Archbishop John Olorunfemi Onaiyekan
Date: October 7, 2009
Code: Classified Top Secret/Circulate on Need to Know Basis

Acknowledging receipt of all brilliant contributions. I defer to the Presidency's superior wisdom that we use the Babangida option and try to settle the Archbishop. I will launch Operation Chop-and-Lets-Chop with immediate effect. As I am acting on the authority of President Yar'Adua and Chief Ogbulafor, I am assuming that I have the full instruments of state at my disposal to bring the operation to fruition. Do I have a liquidity cap?

Cc: Elder Chieftain Stakeholder James Ibori
Chief Michael Aondoakaa (SAN)
Chief Dr Andy Uba

From: Aso Rock
To: PDP National Secretariat and Office of the Senate President
Subject: Archbishop John Olorunfemi Onaiyekan
Date: October 5, 2009
Code: Classified Top Secret/Circulate on Need to Know Basis

President approves Operation Chop-and Lets-Chop with immediate effect. No liquidity cap until the Archbishop is reined in. For limitless liquidity, please refer to Elder James Ibori who has generously agreed to fund the operation. In addition to the carrots of the Babangida method, the President also believes that we should have a contingency stick method. Should the carrot method fail, Ambassador Joe Keshi of Foreign Affairs Ministry has been put on notice to seize the Archbishop's Nigerian passport on any foreign soil when next he ventures out of Nigeria and also deny him Consular Services. Ambassador Keshi is known to be very useful in such missions. Mr. Senate President, please commence the operation immediately.

Cc: Elder Chieftain Stakeholder James Ibori
Chief Michael Aondoakaa (SAN)
Chief Dr Andy Uba

Office of the Senate President of the Federal Republic
National Assembly Complex
Three Arms Zone P.M.B 141 Abuja, Nigeria
Archbishop John Olorunfemi Onaiyekan
Area 3, Section 2, P.O. Box 286, Garki, Abuja, Federal Capital Territory, Nigeria
October 10, 2009

Dear Archbishop Onaiyekan,
I write on behalf of President Yar'Adua and our esteemed party, the PDP, in furtherance of the President's desire to bring respected religious leaders on board in our dogged determination to continue to publicise our intention to eventually launch a seven-point agenda and inaugurate the Rule of Law. As you know, we have recorded spectacular success in the last two years in terms of making Nigerians aware of our impending programmes and prepare them psychologically through the patriotic efforts of our colleague in the Ministry of information, Mrs. Dora Akunyili.

We are now in the phase of reaching out to religious leaders and organisations and I am delighted to inform you that Mr. President is fully aware of your illustrious achievements among the Catholic faithful that you have led so wonderfully since you became Auxiliary Bishop of the Diocese of Ilorin before your current assignment here in Abuja. We are also mindful of the fact that you have been a wonderful seller and rebrander of Nigeria to the international community. Your work speaks for you.

To begin the process of patriotic collaboration with you and the Archdiocese of Abuja, the President has approved a number of friendly measures. First, he has instructed three respected party Elders—Chief James Ibori, Chief Tony Anenih, and Chief Dr Andy Uba—to personally attend the forthcoming thanksgiving Mass of your parish. They will be representing Mr. President and the PDP. Your Lordship, you may begin to put in place the logistics to host these three eminent Nigerians in your church. Contracts have already been awarded for the chairs they will use during Mass. The chairs will be delivered to your church for placement in the front row in due course. Please note that you will need to arrange for a bullion van and significant police escort to immediately take the offertory for that day to the bank. Obviously, because of the presence of the three men, offertory for that day cannot be what you are used to. To this end, the EFCC has been instructed not to get curious should the bank account of the Catholic Archdiocese of Abuja suddenly begin to rival the account of an oil company.

Your Lordship, the President believes that the Catholic Archdiocese of Abuja needs a brand new Basilica. The Cathedral you currently use is not in consonance with the image of the Federal Republic of Nigeria as the Giant of Africa. There is absolutely no reason why the world's biggest Catholic Cathedral should be in Yamoussoukro. As part of our rebranding agenda, Mr. President would like to interest you in the possibility of building a Basilica in Abuja. Not to worry, you have the President's anticipatory approval of import waivers on everything you will need for the project. Customs and Chief Tony Anenih at the NPA are already aware of the fact that the Catholic Church will import huge building materials throughout 2010-2011.

We have also decided to break the monopoly of our trusted and dependable ally on the Lagos-Ibadan expressway in terms of visits for photo-ops by top Federal government functionaries and party elders. Henceforth, you will share such privileges and perks with him. We also believe that you need a private jet in view of your frequent trips to the Vatican to confer with the Pope. To this end, could you please identify five financially healthy members of your church who could be persuaded to obtain a bank loan to buy a jet registered in your name but which they could loan to you every time you need to travel? A friendly bank manager has been instructed to await a loan application from five members of the Catholic Archdiocese of Abuja. Mr. Sanusi Lamido Sanusi has also received clear Presidential instructions not to interfere with the loan process. Needless to say, all taxes on the importation of the jet will be waived. Your jet will also enjoy free parking at the Nnamdi Azikiwe International Airport.

Should you have questions regarding any of these proposals, please be rest assured that I am willing to meet up with you for lunch at the Transcorp Hilton at your convenience.

I await your response.

Yours sincerely,
Major General David Mark (rtd),
Senate President, Federal Republic of Nigeria.

Sjamboks for Governor Ikedi Ohakim

(February 2010)

Dear Governor Ikedi Ohakim,

Greetings from Stellenbosch, South Africa. I write you on behalf of the Commission for the Preservation of Afrikaner Heritage. We have been trying to contact you ever since we received reliable information that you are one Nigerian leader with whom we could potentially do business. Our attempts to get in touch with you through the High Commission of your country in Pretoria were initially unsuccessful as we were told that your High Commissioner, one Alhaji Buba Marwa, now operates from the city of Jeddah in order to be close to his boss. However, the High Commission was quite helpful. They eventually directed us to the BBC in London where we were able to get your address in Owerri, Nigeria.

Although we found it curious that locating a state Governor in Nigeria took us to Jeddah and London, the important thing is that we are now able to write you and establish a regular channel of communication. We are hoping to be able to interest you in a deal that could be mutually beneficial to everyone. On your side, it could enhance your philosophy of governance, leadership, and public service. On ours, we would have the satisfaction of putting part of our history and heritage in the care of someone who truly understands the value of things. If we collaborate successfully, it could also help erase some of the hard feelings generated in your country by our film, *District 9.*

Since you Nigerians know so much about South Africa, it is perhaps not necessary to tell you we, Afrikaners, are not just known for beer and braai. You must know the importance that the sjambok, that heavy leather whip made from hippopotamus or rhinoceros hide, occupies in our history and culture. How could we have brought those uppity and condescending Anglo South Africans under control and keep them in genteel Caucasian resignation, without the symbolic threat that the sjambok represented? Although we hardly ever used it on fellow whites, the possibility of its use kept those arrogant Anglos in their place. And as for the kaffirs—sorry, Black South Africans—how could we have built South Africa on their backs without the sjambok? Today, people from your country come here to salivate over the neon and gloss of our cities: Johannesburg, Pretoria, Cape Town and Durban. But your countrymen hardly ever pause to think that we built those cities by applying the sjambok very scrupulously on kaffirs.

Well, apartheid came to an end. No need to bore you with details you already know. What the rest of the world does not know is that all the talk about rainbow nation or truth and reconciliation masks the cultural genocide that Black South Africa has been perpetuating against us since the end of Apartheid. The ANC, Madiba Nelson Mandela, Thabo Mbeki, and the womanizer currently in power are all guilty. They are allowing some to the symbols of our culture and memory to die. The sjambok is disappearing. You see, a sjambok needs to be used in very specific temperatures on the backs of black people – no offence – or it will begin to rot. Of the 300,000 sjamboks that we had during the sjambok census of 1994, only about 100,000 are left. Because we can no longer use them openly on Black backs in South Africa, we have been looking for a sympathetic African custodian who knows the value of the sjambok.

Nigeria first came to our attention when we learnt that you also have a sjambok culture. Our investigations revealed that you call it koboko and you make it from oxtail or horse tail since you don't have hippos and rhinos in abundance like us. The Nigerian koboko is therefore inferior to the South African sjambok. We were initially discouraged when we investigated the sociology of the koboko in your country. Our feelers in Lagos and Abuja informed us that your *koboko* is mostly used by soldiers and policemen hanging from open trucks to clear ordinary Nigerians from the path of the convoys of your rulers. We didn't see a role for the sjambok in that scenario. Too much sunlight damages the sjambok. We have winter and a generally cooler temperature in South Africa than you have in Nigeria.

Then we heard about you and your personal philosophy of governance by the rod. It is said of you that, as a devout Christian, you do not spare the rod despite minor inconveniences like democracy, human rights and the internet. And if democracy cannot work in Abuja, your capital, we are happy for you that the flagellocracy you have invented is working so well in Imo state. It is said of you that you have been doing a lot of beating, flogging and spanking since you got to Government House in Owerri. It is even said that you started your illustrious career in flogging with a woman. Elizabeth Udoudo was said to have crossed the path of your convoy in the city of Lagos and you had her thoroughly flogged in the street and in the presence of her two children.

But what mostly gladdens the heart is the news that you do most of the flogging in your office where the temperature is cool and controlled. Exactly what we have been looking for! We have a dossier on a journalist called Ikenna Samuelson Iwuoha who, apparently, had the privilege of being flogged by you in your office. It is said that you flogged him an entire day, taking episodic breaks to cool your lungs with pockets of fresh air. We have a file picture of lacerations all over his body. We did our homework.

Your treatment of Mr. Iwuoha and the photo evidence we have sourced to back it up have convinced us that you are our man. What we are proposing is to ship the remaining 100,000 sjamboks in South Africa to you since you know how to make such judicious use of this important symbol of Afrikaner power and history. Rather than suffer the heartbreak of watching them rot away through the cultural genocide of the ANC, we would have the satisfaction of knowing that they are being preserved and used in Nigeria by a man who would have been a very good Afrikaner had providence created him a white South African.

Mr. Governor, if you accept to do us this great favour, we shall award you the Hendrik Verwoerd Medal of Valour. We shall also make you a Life Patron of the Commission for the Preservation of Afrikaner Heritage. This will entitle you to Gold Card participation in an annual secret event we still organise away from the prying eyes of the world. We still hold a yearly kaffir flogging competition. We line up black domestic servants and farm hands and try out new flogging techniques on them. Ever since we heard of your outstanding flogging of Mr. Iwuoha in your office in Owerri, our people have been quite anxious to have you come to Stellenbosch and share your expertise with us.

Yours sincerely,
Eugene Terreblanche,
Senior Sjambok Commissioner,
Commission for the Preservation of Afrikaner Heritage.

Obama for Local Government Chairman

(April 2010)

Dear President Obama,

Apologies for crashing this unsolicited letter into your tight schedule. I am directed by my conscience to write you urgently with regard to your recently disclosed tax returns for the 2009 fiscal year. You and your wife declared a joint annual income of USD 5.5 million out which Uncle Sam sliced USD 1.8 million in taxes.

In essence, the President of the United States and his wife jointly made USD 3.2 million in 2009! The bulk of that money is from book sales and not from your salary and perks of office.

Mr. President, this is truly frustrating and embarrassing. You have only just hosted Goodluck Jonathan, the Acting President of Nigeria. All those ministers, governors and 'miscellaneous aides' you saw grinning from ear to ear behind him are known in Nigerian parlance as his "entourage." Some of those fellas could make your annual income in just one *food for the boys* contract in Abuja. A contract that will never be executed even after full payment has been made upfront.

Some of them could even spend your annual income on a Dubai vacation with a girlfriend—usually an undergraduate sourced for them by aides. Your annual income, Mr. President, is in the region of what an ordinary local government chairman could claim to have spent on "stationery, entertainment, and miscellaneous" in the first quarter of a given fiscal year in Nigeria. If you ever visit Nigeria and spend 24 hours, Mr. President, Aso Rock and the National Assembly could easily invent a supplementary budget way beyond your annual income to host you.

I have given you these background details so that the suggestion I am about to make would not sound outrageous to you. Mr. President, you and Mrs. Obama are wasting time in America. You are violating the message in this Yoruba proverb – *omo to pa owo wale ni iya e nki kaabo* (a mother reserves a special welcome only for the child who brings home sack loads of money). In the spirit of this proverb, I suggest you resign as President of the United States, an office that can only guarantee you less than $5 million a year, and move to Nigeria urgently.

A man of your stature should have no problem becoming a Nigerian citizen within 48 hours. If there are problems, authentic citizenship papers can be arranged very quickly once you land in Lagos. Ask people about *Oluwole*. It is election season in Nigeria and I think you should contest for chairmanship of a local government area.

Mr. President, I am suggesting local government chairmanship because it is the only safe haven left to make dollars in millions in Nigeria. You are a man whose modesty and simplicity are legendary. The money you would make at the local government level would be way beyond what you and Mrs. Obama have ever dreamt of, but you would still be able to maintain your sanity and return to America with enough money to merit that special welcome by Mrs. Obama's mother.

To advise you to run for political office at the state or federal level in Nigeria is to expose you to pure madness. Unfortunately, the madness at those levels is viral and contagious. As governor, rep, senator, minister or Aso Rock hang-around, we are talking of hundreds of millions, or even billions of lootable dollars.

Mr. President, I am not sure that your mental frame could take the idea of being suddenly plunged into the category of the less than 5% of 150 million Nigerians who could make five hundred million dollars in just one deal, have difficulty spending it, and discuss it like chicken change in the public sphere. That is what we are talking about once you venture beyond the local government level that I am recommending. Mind you, a great deal of the money you would make would be loads and loads of raw cash – transported endlessly in what we call *Ghana-*

must-go bags by your aides. If you encounter a man called James Ibori, he will introduce you to the art of ferrying raw cash daily from Nigeria to Dubai; all that cash passing through Nigerian airports unchecked.

This is the sort of vicious, symbolic violence Nigerians have to cope with every day. Violence is the knowledge that not a single Nigerian is able to confidently declare that we have one, just one, elected official anywhere in the country who isn't stealing at the levels I have described. Violence is the kind of figures that are in the newspapers every day: billions and billions being looted in broad daylight by our friends in Abuja and the state capitals. That is terrible knowledge that erodes the sanity of every ordinary Nigerian bit by bit.

Mr. President, if you know that you are going to be able to deal with the quantity of cash available for loot as a governor, rep, senator or Aso Rock insider without losing your mind, then by all means contest for office at those levels. And please do not deceive yourself that you could go there and be principled. The truth of the matter is that every elective office in Nigeria is by nature rigged to turn you into an instant multi-millionaire in dollars.

If you rebel against the nature of your office, Mr. President, if you try to stay above the muck and rot, you will become a clear and present danger to all the Ali Babas around you. They will kill you. So, just go to Nigeria, spend four years *jejely* as a local government chairman, and return to America with the kind of money that will ensure that your two daughters will never have to work.

Yours sincerely,
Professor Tatafo.

Ogbulafor: Thanking God for Little Mercies

(May 2010)

God, I thank you that I am not like other Nigerians – ostriches who do not know how to thank you for little mercies. I thank you for making me the younger brother of the self-righteous Pharisee in Luke 18: 9-14. Apart from fasting twice a week and giving a tenth of everything I earn like my elder brother in the Bible, I am also the only Nigerian thanking you for little mercies in view of Vincent Ogbulafor's recent resignation. God, I thank you for making me realise, unlike other Nigerians, that we do not have the luxury of grumbling that Ogbulafor didn't resign the very moment he was indicted for corruption.

God, I thank you for making me realise, unlike my countrymen and women, that Ogbulafor did something that is so totally un-Nigerian. Those complaining that he took too long to do it, instead of thanking him that he even resigned at all, still don't realise how deep a shit we are in as a nation. Resigning when you are indicted for corruption is a virus that afflicts politicians and public servants in faraway lands like the United States, Canada, Britain, Australia, France, Ghana, Botswana, Benin Republic and South Africa.

You call a quick press conference. Surrounded by your family, friends and soon-to-be-former staff, you announce your resignation because the mere fact of an indictment—whether you end up guilty or not—renders you morally and ethically unfit for public office. You apologise to the public whose confidence you have betrayed and you make promises to commit your life to public good after dealing with the legal consequences of your actions. In such countries, whether you will rise again depends on how well you manage your public act of contrition.

Ogbulafor's peers in the PDP in particular and all Nigerian politicians in general must by now be looking into the immediate, intermediate and remote causes of his betrayal of their class. How did he catch a virus that is so totally un-Nigerian? How could he have done this to them? How could he have gone and set this terrible example? Dimeji Bankole must be cursing Ogbulafor. Were he the leader of parliament in any civilised country, he would not have survived the Peugeot contract scam scandal that he successfully brushed under the carpet. He would have had to call that solemn press conference to announce his resignation the moment the scandal became public knowledge. He knows this. He studied in the UK and is still "forming" all over the place with his nasalised Britico accent as House Speaker in Nigeria. What Dimeji Bankole did is what you do in Nigeria – have your aides (Chief Kay Odunaro and Morgan Omodu) announce that the allegation of corruption is the handiwork of your political enemies and disgruntled elements, hurriedly distribute part of the loot to "stakeholders" and "elder statesmen" you might have initially overlooked, visit Aso Rock three times a week to pledge your unalloyed loyalty to whoever is there, and continue in office in absolute reliance on the short memory of Nigerians.

Senator Joy Emordi is another politician who must be cursing Ogbulafor. She must be wondering why her brother wants to spoil business for her with his bad example of resignation. In the nature of things, being a lawmaker in Nigeria confers on you the special privilege of either breaking the law or simply ignoring it. This explains why the National Assembly is a bazaar, which houses everybody from pedophiles to looters to thugs to bullies. In this context, the little inconvenience of a competent court of law invalidating your election – or at least placing a question mark on it – does not call for resignation. And you can simply count on your fellow moral Lilliputians in the Senate to help you break, avoid, resist or ignore the law. They will never urge you to resign.

God, I must also thank you that Ogbulafor eventually resigned without doing something his fellow corrupt politicians would have expected him to do. He did not run to MASSOB. He did not go to Ohaneze. He did not run to any Eze Igbo of Abuja. He did not attribute his predicament to anti-Igbo elements. He did not say that there is a Hausa/Fulani-Yoruba establishment out there trying to continue the civil war and other genocidal practices against the Igbo by removing him from office. Something must be wrong with that Ogbulafor fellow. Had he played the usual tribal card, it would have been tough to remove him.

God, these are the scenarios Ogbulafor could have explored to remain in office. Unlike other Nigerians, I am thanking you for little mercies because he did not do these things. But precisely because he did not travel that route, I also now suspect that he is not a Nigerian. Because he resigned, my theory now is that his parents must have migrated to Nigeria from Gabon or Equatorial Guinea. He is definitely not a proper Naija politician.

An Unauthorised Biography of Goodluck Jonathan's First Akara

(June 2010)

A witty Yoruba proverb has it that a child wastes the first kobo he earns on akara. Why akara? Don't ask me. I don't know. You never can tell how the ancients came up with some of these proverbs. Like all proverbs, this one is a compressed worldview with a didactic essence. The lesson here is that sudden exposure to real money can make you go gaga. After all, the same Yoruba also say that "anjoonu l'owo" – money is a ghomid. The spirit of money— especially sudden exposure to too much money at the "commanding heights" of the "national cake"— is already at work in Aso Rock, and President Goodluck Jonathan is now "doing *440*" to spend his first kobo on akara.

But this is no ordinary akara. President Jonathan has summoned omo alakara because he has ten billion naira to burn on akara. In case you haven't heard, that is how much Mr. Jonathan proposes to spend on Nigeria's 50th birthday bash. You can always rely on the National Assembly to take expeditious action in matters relating to the belly. They approved Jonathan's supplementary appropriation bill swiftly. Very swiftly. Mind you, supplementary appropriation bill is the botanical name for *more food for the boys* in Abuja. So, the boys in the National Assembly asked no questions whatsoever about the particulars of the akara money. Expectedly, tongues have begun to wag. The internet is abuzz. Reuben Abati and other bewildered columnists are screaming blue murder. If folks are confounded by this mind-boggling budget, they are even more furious about the breakdown.

Here is how the President proposes to spend his akara money. (Warning: patriotic people with heart disease, high blood pressure, or any serious medical condition are advised that this breakdown could aggravate their condition):

- ₦350 million for national unity torch and tour
- ₦ 50 million for Mrs. Patience Jonathan's special visit to special homes, orphanages, prisons, and selected hospitals
- ₦ 20 million for a special session of the National Children Parliament
- ₦ 20 million for a party for 1000 children
- ₦ 40 million for a Presidential banquet
- ₦ 50 million for calisthenics performance
- ₦ 310 million for cultural, historical and military exhibitions
- ₦ 40 million for Food Week
- ₦ 320 million for secretariat equipment, accommodation, logistics, and utilities
- ₦ 30 million for the designing and unveiling of the 50th anniversary logo
- ₦ 1.2 billion for the Ministry of Information and Communications for insertion of special reports on Nigeria in both local and international media
- ₦ 320 million for jingles, adverts, billboards, documentary and publicity
- ₦ 105 million for Ministry of Foreign Affairs for an undisclosed expenditure
- ₦ 700 million for accommodation and transportation of special guests from within and outside the country
- ₦ 450 million for the production of branded souvenirs and gift items for foreign heads of state and to erect the Nigeria Coat of Arms on Aso Rock
- ₦ 210 million for a variety gala night and fireworks

- ₦ 200 million for an international friendly football match and a local competition
- ₦ 120 million naira for event managers and producers
- ₦ 400 million for the publication of a compendium on Nigeria
- ₦ 150 million for a compendium on the Legislature
- ₦ 50 million for a compendium on the Judiciary
- ₦ 10 million for the commissioning of the Golden Jubilee Plaza
- ₦ 540 million for designing, constructing, and mounting a Tower of Unity in the 36 states of the Federation
- ₦ 150 million for debates, essays, conferences, lectures, and a colloquium
- ₦ 60 million for musical concerts and carnivals in the 6 geo-political zones
- ₦ 100 million for durbar, masquerades, and cultural dances
- ₦ 80 million for designing and constructing 10 symbolic monuments of founding fathers of Nigeria.
- ₦ 40 million for a memory tone at the Tafawa Balewa Square, Lagos
- ₦ 500 million for security and protocol
- ₦ 25 million for medicals

Because I am a man with an ear to the ground, I have heard plenty of rumblings from enemies of progress about this budget. Some enemies of our “nascent” and “learning” democracy have described it as pure lunacy. Some say those who sat down in Abuja and came up with this madness aren’t just interested in looting, they say the budget has been designed to shock and awe Nigerians so that the sheer outrageousness of it all will become a distraction from 2011. They say that Nigerians are going to be so pissed they will spend considerable time debating who on earth earmarked 50 million naira to the non-existent office of the First Lady just for Mrs. Jonathan to visit orphanages and prisons during the celebrations!

I have also overheard some other bellyachers say that undesignated looting went by the official name of “miscellaneous expenses” in our vocabulary of corruption but this budget has invented a new and more ambitious vocabulary – "undisclosed expenditure." The Foreign Affairs Ministry will test run this new addition to our vocabulary of corruption by spending 105 million of our naira as "undisclosed expenditure" during the party. The naysayers are claiming that the lootapalooza that has been packaged as our 50th anniversary budget is so dizzying, so gargantuan, so brazen that nobody will remember to remain vigilant about what the usual suspects may be up to in the build-up to 2011. Uncharitable as ever, these naysayers are now calling the budget a lunatic weapon of mass distraction.

I disagree with them. I have a different take on this akara budget. No matter how horrible Nigeria's rulership has been since independence, there are some past rulers who could still claim to have invested massively in infrastructure with the "change" they had left after looting the bulk of the oil money. Somebody somewhere can say: "I developed Lagos. All those bridges and flyovers are my legacy. Never mind that I told the world that how to spend money was our problem. We were all drunk during that oil boom. The bridges of Lagos are my legacy." There are also some rulers who, between them, could say: "We built Abuja from the scratch. Abuja is our legacy from the Niger Delta's oil money."

Methinks President Jonathan wants to sit down quietly somewhere in Bayelsa, twenty years from now, and declare solemnly: "My legacy? I partied. The first ten billion I had from the oil money, I blew it on *akara*. I organised that historic and gigantic owambe party to mark Nigeria's 50th birthday. Africa's most expensive party organised by Africa's biggest political party. That is my legacy." We don't know if President Jonathan will contest; if he does, we can pretend not to know that the dynamics of incumbency would grant him (s)election success. Therefore, we have to assume for the sake of argument that this is the only shot he has on that seat. We have to assume that this will be the only providential shot of the Niger Delta in the next two life times. We have to assume that rather than attempt to build a city like Abuja somewhere in the Niger Delta—at least start it—and damn the consequences, Mr. Jonathan has decided that a ten-billion owambe party would be his lasting legacy.

As a patriotic Nigerian, I have some suggestions to help him consolidate this emergent legacy. I think he needs to add two billion naira only to that budget to take care of some critical omissions that I have noticed. If you budget 700 million naira for transportation and accommodation of domestic and foreign guests (looks like they plan to buy new planes to fly in their guests), it goes without saying that kidnappers would see the foreign guests as prime target. Because of the total collapse of modern structures of policing, discipline, and punishment in Nigeria, the Oba of Benin has had to go back to ancestral methods of dealing with kidnappers. A ritual was recently performed at his behest in Benin, and kidnappers were cursed ancestrally. I hear it is working because our superstitious people fear original African taboo more than they fear the white man's law and order. I propose we earmark one billion naira for the Oba of Benin for special cursing rituals starting from September 25, 2010. The curse should target any kidnapper hoping to embarrass the Federal Government by kidnapping visiting Heads of State or Hollywood stars invited to the owambe anniversary. That brings us to 11 billion naira.

President Jonathan recently had a stopover in Saudi Arabia on his way home from France. He wanted to thank the king of that country for taking care of our late President but was told that the king was "not on seat." Well, we have many countries to thank as part of our 50th anniversary. Ever since our rulers gave our country to the dogs and created a national archetype called Andrew in the 1980s, the developed countries of Euro-America have played host to that character. They've had to deal with all the national traits and stereotypes of a character running away from lack of water, electricity, security, and other basic necessities of life in Nigeria, the "giant of Africa."

By the 1990s, countries like Benin Republic, Burkina Faso, Ghana, Botswana, Swaziland, Lesotho, South Africa, China, Japan, India, Bangladesh, Malta, Saudi Arabia, Sudan, Ethiopia, Eritrea, Vietnam, Thailand, Ukraine, Nepal, Iraq, Afghanistan, Pakistan, Azerbaijan, Papua New Guinea and Kenya joined the regulars in Europe and

North America in hosting and coping with the voluntary economic refugees produced by Nigeria`s fifty years of colossal failure. These countries have had to deal and cope with new economies of meaning associated, fairly or unfairly, with our presence. As part of our 50th owambe celebration, I propose a budget of one billion naira only for a Presidential delegation to visit and thank all the countries that have hosted and taken care of Andrew all these years. The roving Thank You Delegation should be headed by Ojo Maduekwe. Micheal Aondoakaa, Tafa Balogun, James Ibori, Patricia Etteh, Tanimu Yakubu and Bukola Saraki should be members of that delegation. That brings us to twelve billion naira only.

Now, if President Jonathan spends ten billion (plus my suggested 2 billion) on akara and does not get the chance to be in the saddle after 2011 in order to do other things that could add up to a concrete legacy, we all know that history's harsh judgment awaits him. Nigerians will talk forever about the most expensive celebration of fifty years of absolute state failure the world has ever seen; his people in the Niger Delta will accuse him forever of squandering their only shot at the "national cake" on akara.

When this happens, he will need to explain things to his people by re-writing history. That is the nature of Nigerian rulers. After messing up, they always try to smuggle themselves into nice corners of our history "before our very before." Witness how much Babangida has spent on hagiographers since 1993. And we know that in the nature of things in Nigeria, the other, especially the ethnic other, is always responsible for one's poor choices. If an Igbo man coughs in the morning, those *ngbati* and *ofem manu* traitors and bastards are responsible; if a Yoruba man farts in the afternoon, those stingy *inyanminrin* bastards are responsible; if the Igbo and the Yoruba pee in the evening, those illiterate and uncivilised mallams in the north are responsible; if the Fulani man has a headache at night, those filthy infidels who are not born to rule in the west and the east are responsible. No Nigerian ethnic group is ever responsible for anything.

This national malaise explains why I pity the two Yoruba people who are Minister of Finance and Minister of State for Finance respectively in President Jonathan's cabinet at the moment. When history begins to snarl furiously at the retired Goodluck Jonathan some twenty years down the road, I foresee and predict the following conversation:

History: Jonathan, you had a golden opportunity and you blew it partying. Why on earth did you spend your first ten billion naira on akara when you could have spent just under a billion on credible electoral reform and given the country a fresh start in electoral ethos? What a legacy that would have been! You would have written your name in gold but you opted for a ten billion *owambe*.

Goodluck Jonathan: *Hmm, my broda, see me o.* I made the mistake of appointing two Yoruba people in the Ministry of Finance. They made me do it. They said it was o.k. They said that we could afford the grandiose party. You know Yoruba people and *owambe*.

2011 National Honours List: The Preparation Memos

(October 2010)

From: President and Commander-in-Chief of the Armed Forces, Federal Republic of Nigeria
To: Federal Cabinet; Cabal; PDP Godfathers, Chieftains, Stakeholders, and Elder Statesmen
Topic: Preparation of the 2011 National Honours List
Status: Need-to-know

I, Dr. Goodluck Ebele Azikiwe Jonathan, President and Commander-in-Chief of the Armed forces of the Federal Republic of Nigeria, am directed to notify you all of my intention to commence broad-based consultations towards drawing up a provisional list of meritorious and credible Nigerians for the 2011 National Honours list. You are all aware of the premium that my administration places on the national honours programme. To the glory of God, my administration successfully organised the 2010 awards ceremony during which beloved compatriots such as Chief Mrs. Patricia Etteh, Mr. Femi Otedola, Alhaji Dikko Inde and Mr. Ogbonnaya Onovo were rewarded for their illustrious and selfless service to this great country of ours. We must consolidate and sustain this solid foundation after winning the 2011 election. I can think of no other way to celebrate our anticipated landslide victory in the forthcoming election than to honour another set of eminent and illustrious Nigerians. To this end, may I seize this opportunity to call on you, members of the Executive Council of the Federation, my kitchen cabinet or cabal, loyal Aso Rock aides, Godfathers, Chieftains, Stakeholders, and Elder Statesmen within our great party, to nominate prospective awardees and commence a vigorous debate in order to ensure that we put forward and honour only the best amongst us.

From: Federal Cabinet; Cabal; PDP Godfathers, Chieftains, Stakeholders, and Elder Statesmen
To: President and Commander-in-Chief of the Armed Forces, Federal Republic of Nigeria
Topic: Preparation of the 2011 National Honours List
Status: Need-to-know

Your Excellency, Dr. Goodluck Ebele Azikiwe Jonathan, President and Commander-in-Chief of the Armed Forces of the Federal Republic of Nigeria, we, members of the Executive Council of the Federation, your kitchen cabinet or cabal, loyal Aso Rock aides, Godfathers, Chieftains, Stakeholders, and Elder Statesmen in the PDP, wish to thank you for the confidence reposed in us as we begin the nomination process for the 2011 national honours. This, Your Excellency, is yet another demonstration of your unflinching determination to mend Nigeria and move the country forward. Upon reception of your brilliant memo, Your Excellency sir, we immediately formed various committees and strategy caucuses to streamline the nomination process. Chief among these are the Nominations Collection and Collation Committee, the Nominations Vetting Committee, the Facebook Liaison Committee which we charged to seek the input of your teeming Facebook constituency, the Religious Harmony Committee to ensure a fair representation of Christians and Muslims in the final list, and the Ethnic Equity Committee to ensure equal representation of Yoruba, Hausa, and Igbo in the lit. Sorry, your Excellency sir, we meant Ijaw, Yoruba, Hausa, and Igbo. In line with the spirit of democracy sir, these committees have been empowered to form their own subcommittees. We shall submit periodic progress reports to the Presidency.

From: President and Commander-in-Chief of the Armed Forces, Federal Republic of Nigeria
To: Federal Cabinet; Cabal; PDP Godfathers, Chieftains, Stakeholders, and Elder Statesmen
Topic: Preparation of the 2011 National Honours List
Status: Need-to-know

Your last memo refers. I, Dr. Goodluck Ebele Azikiwe Jonathan, President and Commander-in-Chief of the Armed Forces of the Federal Republic of Nigeria, am delighted by your speedy reaction to my directive on the national awards process. I have therefore directed the Minister for Special Duties to coordinate the activities of the committees that you have formed while the Minister of Special Duties will liaise with the corresponding subcommittees. Be assured that the Presidency is ready to provide further assistance for the speedy completion of your work. To this end, a mobilisation sum of five billion naira has been anticipatorily approved for your immediate, intermediate, and remote expenses in the course of this onerous national assignment.

From: Federal Cabinet; Cabal; PDP Godfathers, Chieftains, Stakeholders, and Elder Statesmen
To: President and Commander-in-Chief of the Armed Forces, Federal Republic of Nigeria
Topic: Preparation of the 2011 National Honours List
Status: Need-to-know

Your Excellency, Dr. Goodluck Ebele Azikiwe Jonathan, President and Commander-in-Chief of the Armed Forces of the Federal Republic of Nigeria, we are delighted to inform you that after several months of rigorous and painstaking work, our various committees and subcommittees have now drawn up a provisional list of ten illustrious

Nigerians for your kind consideration for the 2011 national honours. Your Excellency sir, the following men and women made the cut:

Dr. Andy Uba
Professor Maurice Iwu
Alhaji Salisu Buhari
Alhaji Senator Sani Ahmed Yerima
Hon. Dimeji Bankole
Hon. Ndidi Elumelu
Hon. Dino Melaye
Chief Mrs. Cecilia Ibru
Chief Olabode George
Dr. Amos Adamu

Mr. President Sir, these are, of course, just the first ten outstanding names. Our list was drawn using the excellent criteria and parametres that appear to have informed your choice of awardees in the 2010 calendar: probity, integrity, honesty, character, hard work, and selfless service to Nigeria. We realise that Chief Olabode George and Chief Mrs. Cecilia Ibru are currently in less than complimentary circumstances but we feel very strongly that our great party owes them one. Ours is a party of trickle-down prosperity and the story of that philosophy of ours cannot be told without mentioning the enormous contributions of Chiefs Bode George and Cecilia Ibru to the history of prosperity in this country since 1999. In foreign affairs, at no time have relations between Nigeria and the Arab world been stronger. This is especially true of relations between Nigeria and Egypt. We achieved this feat largely through the patriotic efforts of Alhaji Senator Sani Ahmed Yerima, hence his inclusion in the provisional list. Mr. President Sir, we wish to commend the Minister for Special Duties and the Minister of Special Duties. These two members of your cabinet were of immense help to our committees. The story of sports in Nigeria is the story of Dr. Amos Adamu. We believe that he has now shown himself worthy of a national award. There is no better time to honour this great son of Nigeria than now.

From: President and Commander-in-Chief of the Armed Forces, Federal Republic of Nigeria
To: Federal Cabinet; Cabal; PDP Godfathers, Chieftains, Stakeholders, and Elder Statesmen
Topic: Preparation of the 2011 National Honours List
Status: Need-to-know

Your last memo refers. I, Dr. Goodluck Ebele Azikiwe Jonathan, President and Commander-in-Chief of the Armed Forces of the Federal Republic of Nigeria, write to thank you all for your service. You have done an excellent job and I am absolutely delighted that you have come up with such a fantastic list of great and outstanding Nigerians. I wholeheartedly endorse your list. I am particularly pleased that you have stated the need for us to support our brother, Dr. Amos Adamu, by giving him a national honour. He is an outstanding Nigerian and a friend of our great party who will surely survive the attempts to pull him down by the enemies of our country. I will forward your list to the National Council of State with immediate effect and I have no doubt in my mind that it will sail through easily. God bless the Federal Republic of Nigeria.

Ghana and the Road to Nigeria

(December 2010)

To the accompaniment of Phil Collins's "That's Just the Way it is."

Dear Ghana,

Last week, you officially became a very important country in world geo-politics as you joined the league of oil-producing countries. The first gush of oil came after a ceremony attended by President John Atta Mills. I would have advised President Atta Mills and every member of Ghana's leadership to travel to a village called Oloibiri in Nigeria and read what is written on the withered foreheads of the villagers – before pumping that epochal first drop of Ghanaian oil. It would have been a sobering learning experience for them. Anyway, welcome to the world of Nigeria, Angola and Gabon. Now that you are no longer just a backyard producer of cocoa and gold, you will begin to notice significant shifts in how you are treated by the international community – defined as the countries of Western Europe and America. You see, in international relations, all men were not created equal. The rule here is Orwellian: the owner of black gold is infinitely more equal than the owner of gold and cocoa. Don't even mention groundnut sellers like Senegal. They are not on the radar and will not be, until the Americans discover in the future that groundnut contains ingredients that could cure obesity. That's the way it is. That's just the way it is.

Here are the early indications of your new status that you must watch out for: you will be promoted from occasional spectator status to enhanced spectator status during G8 and G20 summits; President Atta Mills will be invited to Washington in the first quarter of 2011 on a grand state visit, and White House chefs will be taught to prepare gourmet kenkey; your Ambassador in Washington will suddenly become a very important man and will begin to receive lots of invitations to White House dinners much to the displeasure of Nigeria and South Africa; your Ambassador will soon become the Dean of the African diplomatic corps in Washington. That's the way it is. That's just the way it is.

Hillary Clinton will now regularly mention a special relationship that has always existed between Ghana and the USA in her speeches. Her speechwriters will arrange for more than 50% of African Americans to trace their root to a village near the Akosombo dam in 2011. Luckily, African Americans tend to discover and locate their roots wherever the wind of augury is blowing in Africa. Many of them discovered their Zulu and Xhosa ancestry when South Africa was the talk of the town in 1994. Oprah Winfreh may now announce that she is no longer of Zulu heritage but her ancestors were actually proud Akan warriors. And the brand new Reverend Al Sharpton Okomfo Anokye Junior may announce an emotional trip home to his roots in Kumasi. Hillary Clinton may start carrying a kente handbag in her public appearances; President Obama may now suddenly remember that his father's family actually migrated from Ghana to Kenya sometime in the 19th century; some lunatic Republican Senator may declare loudly in Congress, "We are all Ghanaians!" People from Guyana in South America should expect their enlightened American neighbours or colleagues at work to say, "Hey buddy, I heard that your African country now has oil. Good for ya!" That's the way it is. That's just the way it is.

There is more. Before the middle of 2011, the State Department will suddenly discover an old memo recommending the construction of a bigger and more functional American embassy in Accra that will rival the embassies in Baghdad and Kabul in size; before the end of 2011, AFRICOM commanders will recommend the establishment of a major

Accra substation and Green Zone to pre-emptorily break the linkages between Ghanaian terrorists and their newly-discovered Ashanti relatives in the rugged regions of Yemen, Pakistan and Afghanistan; China, as usual, will do her job more quietly and effectively than the noisy Americans to make sure that your black gold comes under the red flag and not the star-spangled banner. In other words, you own that oil the way a child in Africa is said to own a goat that he feeds and cares for only to discover the true owner of the goat the day it is slaughtered and he gets the entrails while the elders in the compound feast on the real meat. Somewhere between America and China, you will soon know who the real owners of the oil are. That's the way it is. That's just the way it is.

For now, the oil companies running the show are unknown British and American quantities called Tullow Oil Plc and Kosmos Energy LLC. Exxon Mobil is said to have sniffed around like a dog and walked out on a deal to buy Kosmos Energy's share of the new booty in Ghana. That is because it is still morning yet in Ghana's oil destiny. Don't worry. ExxonMobil will be back. They always come back. The other big boys will also descend on Ghana once they secure China's permission: BP, Shell, Chevron, Total Elf, and ConocoPhillips. I'm afraid the arrival of all these people will mark the official end of the independence you got in 1957. They will establish and run parallel governments in Accra complete with their own sovereign armed forces that will have the right to shoot down your citizens in broad daylight if they are deemed obstacles to pipelines. Henceforth, no one will win presidential elections in Ghana without their say-so. Five years from now, watch out for Wikileaks's release of conversations between the American Ambassador in Accra and the CEOs of these Western oil companies. They will talk about Ghana's president like an obedient school boy. That's the way it is. That's just the way it is.

My dear Ghana, please do not be distracted by these little things. Washington, Beijing and the oil companies are the least of your problems. Your real problem now is Abuja. I am sure you know that little story about the road to hell being infinitely more attractive than the road to salvation? Hell, for you Ghana, is Abuja. Abuja is inhabited by an irresponsible political rulership that has done with Nigeria's oil everything you should not do with your own oil. Whatever you do, do not take the road to Abuja with your oil. It is a sure road to perdition. You want to make sure you go the way of the United Arab Emirates with your oil. I am writing, therefore, to help you develop an early warning signal based on the colour codes developed by the Americans in the age of terrorism. The mechanism I am advocating will help you determine how dangerously close to Abuja you are at any point and quickly retrace your steps. That's the way it is. That's just the way it is.

You need to pay attention to the language of your citizens. The fumes of oil are worse than the fumes of alcohol. Oil inebriates in a far more lethal fashion. Your citizens may start using words, phrases and sentences hitherto unknown in Ghanaian English. Monitor and police them closely. When regular Joes, sorry, regular Mensahs, suddenly begin to gather in Kwame Nkrumah Circle or Labadi beach in Accra to talk about "resource control", that is bad news. Not good at all. You should put your warning signal in code yellow when this happens. From resource control, your politicians and public officials may suddenly begin to make a lot of noise about "onshore" and "offshore" dichotomy. When you begin to hear talk like that, put your alarm system in code orange. That's the way it is. That's just the way it is.

Watch your parliamentarians. They are not unaware of what their irresponsible counterparts are doing in the National Assembly in Abuja. It's just that cocoa and gold could not in any way have guaranteed parity of extravagance with Abuja. Now that there is oil, parliamentary discourse in Accra may suddenly be exclusively reduced to the following keywords: estacode, upward budget review, upward contract review, supplementary appropriation, constituency projects, hardship allowances, newspaper allowances, furniture allowances, recharge card allowances, convoy allowances, renovation allowances, anticipatory approvals. I pity and fear for the Cedi. She will become an endangered species in the language of your politicians and government officials once the petrodollars begin to flow. They will carry out all their transactions in dollars and frown whenever Cedis are mentioned. They may begin to stash raw dollar bills in the presidential Castle in Accra. When all this happens, you are still in code orange. That's the way it is. That's just the way it is.

Watch out for the Big Brother and "Giant of Africa" disease. It is worse than HIV/AIDS and it has no cure. You see, oil is at once sociology and pathology. Behind every irresponsible national elite in Africa, there is plenty of oil. And you must know that while Nigeria's national elite may be the king of irresponsibility, they have no monopoly over it. Your politicians and the new oil elite in Accra may forget that there is still hunger in Ho and Hohoe and begin to ship loads of dollars to places like Chad, Guinea, Niger Republic, Mali, Burkina Faso, Liberia, Gambia, Mauritania, the Congos and Sierra Leone. Rivalry with Nigeria being an ever-present stimulus, they may get ambitious and begin to fund every peacekeeping operation in the continent. They may even begin to tell ECOWAS and the AU that Ghana's problem is not money but how to spend it. When this happens, Ghana is already in the outskirts of Abuja, approaching downtown Abuja at breakneck speed. That's the way it is. That's just the way it is.

If you want to travel the Big Brother route with your new petrodollars, you must always remember that no matter how much you give in aid to fellow African countries, your citizens will be the first to be stereotyped and spat upon when they visit those recipient countries. Well, you already know how you treat Nigerians in Ghana these days so we are not in strange territory here. And you know that our friends in South Africa now see a *makwerekwere* in every Nigerian despite millions of petrodollars sunk into the anti-apartheid struggle by Nigeria. Very soon, our friends in Uganda, Tanzania and Kenya will erect airport showers to disinfect the Nigerians they grudgingly allow into those countries after frisking worse than any indignity an African could suffer in a Euro-American airport. And remember that Ellen Johnson Sirleaf ran to Washington to thank them for money and limbs that Nigeria lost while preserving her country even as the unconcerned Americans watched the carnage on TV with their hamburgers and Budweisers in hand, between the NBA and the Super Bowl. It is not certain that Mama in Monrovia even remembers that Abuja spent the money to defend and later patch up her country, not Washington. Those are the little indignities of big brotherhood in Africa that you must be prepared for as you begin to flex some muscle with your oil. That's the way it is. That's just the way it is.

You want to ensure that things do not reach code red by which time your citizens will be talking of MEER – Movement for the Emancipation of Every Region. Somewhere above the cacophony of Kalashnikovs, a stupid oil billionaire may even announce publicly to Ghanaians that he does not know what to do with the five hundred million dollars he just made in profit from the sale of a single oil block. Once you get to this stage, it is too late. That's the way it is. That's just the way it is.

Part Two:

In the Beginning was the Word

Oruka

(September 2009)

And it came to pass that a great urge to sleep for four years fell on Moloch Yaddie, ruler of the land Sodom, for his eyes were heavy. And he saith unto his Sanhedrin: "Lo, I go to sleep for four years. Appoint one of thineself even now who shall tender the vineyard, take care of thee, and make a beautiful bride for my son in whom I am well pleased. Make haste for my great sleep is at hand." And it came to pass that there was great rejoicing among the Sanhedrin for one of them was going to tender the vineyard and marry the anointed son while Moloch Yaddie slept. This was not strange, for in the land of Sodom, men marry men and women marry women.

And it came to pass that the Sanhedrin sought counsel saying: "Who shall we choose to tender Moloch Yaddie's vineyard and marry his anointed son?" And it came to pass that the wisdom of Baal, their god, fell upon them whereupon they selected a very dark man named Aondokelech the Tivite. And it came to pass that Aondokelech the Tivite approached the throne of Moloch Yaddie to pay obeisance, saying: "Oh great Moloch, even as it pleaseth thee, I will tender thine vineyard and marry thine anointed son." And it came to pass that Moloch Yaddie looked unto the Tivite and asked: "Why art thou so dark?" And the Tivite replied: "Oh great Moloch, look not down upon me because I am black, because the sun hath looked upon me." And Moloch Yaddie was pleased with this answer full of the wisdom of Baal. And he saith unto the Tivite: "My vineyard thou shalt tender but art thou worthy of my son? Doest thou even knoweth his story?"

And it came to pass that Aondokelech the Tivite replied with much wisdom, saying: "Oh great Moloch, thine loving son, Iborilech the Edomite, was originally from the land of Gomorrah. He was pushed out of Gomorrah by his real father for it was said that Iborilech was of light fingers because his mother was the sister of one of the forty thieves who lived in Ali Baba's cave in the land of the Arabs. But he found favour in thine eyes when he came to Sodom and thou adopted him as thine anointed son." And it came to pass that Moloch Yaddie was very pleased with the wisdom of the Tivite and he ordered a great banquet to join his son, Iborilech the Edomite, and Aondokelech the Tivite together in holy matrimony.

And it came to pass that there was great rejoicing in the land of Sodom. And they called a great feast to celebrate the wedding. Iborilech the Edomite and Aondokelech the Tivite looked truly regal on their wedding day. Kings and Ambassadors of every land in the world came, bearing gifts of great value for the new couple. And the members of the Sanhedrin, possessed of wine, spake and sang in tongues, as the couple marched through the streets of Sodom in a procession of splendour. They sang in a strange tongue, saying:

Oruka ti d'owo na
Di ololufe re mu
Ko s'eni to le ya yin
Titi lai lai

And it came to pass that Iborilech the Edomite and Aondokelech the Tivite danced to this strange song to celebrate their union. And it came to pass that the hedonists finished the wine by midnight. And there was great anger in the household of Moloch Yaddie for the ruler had paid for the wine to last until dawn. And it came to pass that there was a man named Victory, who came from a lineage of people who believed in the dignity of the crown. For a very long time Victory was a lowly scribe who wrote for the people of Sodom against the rulers who oppressed them. But he found favour with the crown even as it is written in his father's name and was invited to the Rock to be the official loudspeaker of Moloch Yaddie. And Victory came unto his Master and said: "Oh great Moloch, let it be known that I inherited twenty-five drums of wine from my father which I now give freely to the new royal couple."

And it came to pass that there was a woman named Dora the wine taster who was from the tribe of the black Israelites enlightened by half of a yellow sun. And Dora the wine taster savoured the new wine, turned to Victory the loudspeaker who gaveth the wine, and said: "Every man at the beginning doth set forth good wine, and when men have well drunk, then that which is worse. But thou hast kept the good wine until now. Let this wine be rebranded as the mark of the giantness of the land of our father Moloch Yaddie."

And it came to pass that after the great feast and when Moloch Yaddie hath gone into the great sleep that would last four years, Aondokelech the Tivite went unto his new bride but could not know him for Iborilech the Tivite was troubled. And Aondokelech the Tivite asked of his new bride: "What trouble besiege thee that I cannot know thee on the night of our union? Would thou maketh me Onan?"

And it came to pass that Iborilech the Edomite opened his mouth and spake thus: "Oh Aondokelech my lover, mine heart is heavy for the Queen of the kingdom of Anglosalem accuses me of storing thirty six million shekels of my father's money in her land. The shekels belong to the land of Sodom. What belongeth to the land of Sodom belongeth to my father, Moloch Yaddie. What belongeth to my father is my inheritance."

And it came to pass that Aondokelech the Tivite saith unto his troubled bride: "Fear not. I am with thee. No weapon fashioned against thee by thine enemies shall prosper. A thousand shall fall by thine right hand, twenty thousand shall fall by thine left hand, they shall not harm even a hair of thine head. Only with thine eyes shalt thou see the iniquities of thine enemies. For I will rise tomorrow and go forth to the land of Anglosalem and tell their Queen, 'Touch not my anointed!' Sleep well now, my love."

And it came to pass that as the royal couple slept, drunk members of the Sanhedrin were heard making merry and singing until the early hours of the morning the theme song of the great wedding:

Oruka ti d'owo na
Di ololufe re mu
Ko s'eni to le ya yin
Titi lai lai

Theophilus' Portion

(March 2010)

And it came to pass that during the reign of King Achab the Kanurite over the land of Sodom, a man named Theophilus the warrior found favour in the eyes of the great ruler.

And Achab summoned Theophilus and saith: "Lo, thou has been a faithful servant of the Chosen tribe that lies to the north of the great river. The time has come to reward thee according to the deeds of thine hands."

And Achab took Theophilus to the top of a mountain from whence their eyes fell upon the sprawling riches of the lands to the deep South of the great river. And Achab saith unto Theophilus: "Behold the black gold to the south of the great river. All this I will give thee if thou wilt fall down and worship me." And Theophilus cast himself on the ground and did obeisance, saying: "Thou art worthy, o my God, to receive glory and honour and power. For thou hast taken all the black gold and for thine pleasure it was created."

And Achab was pleased, for Theophilus hath called him God. And he saith unto Theophilus: "Possess now thine possession. Go forth from this mountain and take dominion over any well of black gold in the south of the great river that pleases thine heart. That shall be thine portion in thine father's house." And Theophilus went forth to his well, singing hymns of praise.

And when he hath taken possession of his well of black gold, Theophilus made haste to go to Jerusalem, for he hath need to go to the temple in search of moneychangers. And when the moneychangers saw him, they fled, for fear came upon them. But Theophilus saith unto them: "Fear not. I have not come to flog and drive you out of here like the Nazarene carpenter. I come in peace." Whereupon the moneychangers saith: "What then is thine heart's desire?" And Theophilus saith unto them: "Lo, I have found favour in the eyes of Achab the Kanurite, ruler of the land of Sodom, and he hath given me a well of black gold. I now wish to sell my inheritance, for I am told that the land of Jerusalem hath only olives and no black gold."

And there was great rejoicing among the moneychangers. Whereupon they decided to buy the well. And they came unto Theophilus and saith: "Make merry, eat and drink with us. After the feast, we shall wash thine feet and ye shall lie down to sleep. Tomorrow, we shall give thee five hundred million shekels for thine well of black gold."

And Theophilus returned to the land of Sodom with five hundred million shekels, but change hath come upon the land of his birth. Achab the Kanurite had died. His friend, King Ahasuerus, who hath reign from India even unto Ethiopia over a hundred and twenty and seven provinces, hath sent him two women. It was said that Achab the Kanurite died after going into the two women. Theophilus was sad, for he had hoped that King Achab would teach him what to do with his five hundred million shekels.

And it came to pass that rulers worse than the terrible Achab came upon Sodom. And the people cursed their God, saying: "We shout thine name more than any other people on earth; we built the mightiest temple on earth unto thee on the great road to the great city by the sea, yet thou afflict us with evil rulers. And though we walk through the valley of the shadow of death, thine rod and thine staff we see not." And because they cursed Him, I Am That I Am caused the plagues from the land of Egypt and the afflictions of the man called Job to migrate to the land of Sodom. Hunger, pestilence and desolation struck the Sodomites.

And the people began to die for they hath no shekels. A thousand fell by the right hand of Theophilus, ten thousand fell by his left hand. And the living-dead and the dead-living screamed: "Give us shekels to buy food, lest we perish of hunger." But Theophilus could not hear them, for he was far gone in spirit. And in spirit he saw a powerful vision of the second coming of Achab the Kanurite, who would come in rapturous revelation, to teach him what to do with the five hundred million shekels he hath hidden under a bushel. So let it be written, so let it be done.

Tongues for Nigeria

(April 2010)

Oh shantara ma ma ma ma ma ma! Oh shantara ma ma ma ma ma ma! Oh shantara ma ma ma ma ma! Daddy Jehovah Jireh in heaven! Oh yantana ma ma ma ma ma! Daddy we bless you and magnify your holy name, for you are God. Daddy we glorify you, for you are worthy to be praised. Daddy, we worship you for this is the day that you have made and you have anointed us to rejoice and be glad in it. Daddy, we thank you for making us the power and the force of your word. For you promised us that whatsoever we bind here in this sinful world, even that shall ye bind in heaven.

Oh shantara ma ma ma ma ma ma! Father, we bind the spirit of paedophilia in our land. Father we come against the demons of paedophilia. Father we call on your authority and we know that you will answer by fire. For it was you who came against the demons of the Gerasene demoniacs and cast them into pigs. Father, we ask you to come against the demons of paedophilia in our errant son, Sani Ahmed Yerima, and cast them into donkeys for there are no pigs in his sharia land in Zamfara. Father, we call upon thee to burn his demons and render his loins weak even before he goes into the 13 year-old girl he has just bought from the land of the Pharaohs.

Oh yantana ma ma ma ma ma ma ma! Oh shantara ma ma ma ma ma ma! He is God/He is God amen/He has risen from the dead/ He is God/ Every knee shall bow/ Every tongue confess/ That Jesus Christ is God! Oh shantara ma ma ma ma ma ma! Father, we come against the principalities and powers of impotence and unmanliness in our land. For it was given unto us to make a man of Goodluck Jonathan, O Lord! But he lives in fear of a ghost and the wife of the ghost, O Lord. He is unable to sanctify the house of power against the presence of the ghost, O Lord. And the wife of the ghost is made man over him.

Oh yantana ma ma ma ma ma ma ma! Father we call upon you to rain energy into Goodluck Jonathan's loins, courage into his heart, and spine into his back, so that he can become a man. Father, you led by example. For it was you who assumed power, flogged, arrested and drove those corrupt moneychangers out of thine temple in Jerusalem. Father, Goodluck Jonathan hath eyes but cannot see thine example; though he hath ears, he doth not hear of thine leadership by example. Hence a rogue moneychanger called James Ibori has been defiling the temple called Nigeria under Jonathan's watch. The cavalry of Ibori has successfully defied Jonathan and his centurion, Ogbonaya Onovo, just because Jonathan is not yet a man. Father, render unto him the strength of a lion, for you are the lion of the tribe of Judah. We remove and bind the dominion of effeminacy in Jonathan's life in the m-i-g-h-t-y name of J-e-s-u-s! Oooooooooooh! Oooooooooooo! Oh yantana ma ma ma ma ma ma ma! Oh shantara ma ma ma ma ma ma! I feel it now! I feel the spirit in me now! It has descended. It is raining/ All around me/I can feel it/All around me.

Thank you, Lord. You are able/ Abundantly able/ To deliver, to deliver/ You are able/Abundantly able/ To deliver those who trust in thee. Oh shantara ma ma ma ma ma ma! Father, the Nigerian nation trusts in thee. They call on thee more than any other nation on earth. Some of them call on thee before they loot. Some call on thee before they give or accept bribe. Armed robbers commit their goings and comings unto thine hands. Hired assassins call on thee before stepping out. Nigerians pray in their offices and preach your word in secular Internet forums. Father in heaven, we ask you to look with favour on the prayers and ministrations of this religious people and make a Saul of them.

Oooooooooooh! Oooooooooooo! Oh yantana ma ma ma ma ma

ma ma! Oh shantara ma ma ma ma ma ma! Father, Nigerians need to become Saul, for an Amalekite called Ibrahim Babangida wants to come upon them a second time. Father Lord, you know the story of the first coming of this Amalekite in the lives of this people. For the eight years that he ruled them, birds did not chirp like birds, rats did not brux like rats, and men did not speak like men. He brought pestilence upon the land, O Lord. And even unto this day, his heart is hardened like the heart of Pharaoh for he has refused to wear sackcloth and apologise for his sins. Oh Lord, we pray that the Saul of Nigeria brings the abomination of desolation to bear on the ambition of this mad Amalekite.

Father, we thank you for you have listened to our prayers.

Father, we thank you for you have answered our prayers in the mighty name of Jesus!! A-m-e-n!!!! Hello somebody! Hello Pastor Pius! Turn to your neighbour and say: "Your prayer has been answered!"

Mene, Mene, Tekel, Upharsin

(June 2010)

And it came to pass that, for a second time since he stepped aside from the throne of his fathers, Badamasi the Minnarite, whose house sitteth atop a hill, desired to reclaim that throne, for it was given unto the cattle rearers of his tribe to claim dominion over all the other tribes in the land – starting from the tribe of the merrymakers in the west to the tribe of the black Jews in the east and the tribe of the hewers-but-not-partakers-of-black-gold in the deep South.

And Badamasi summoned all the princes of the tribe of cattle rearers and saith unto them: "Behold, death hath looked upon our brother who was named after the Prophet Musa and placed the throne of our fathers in the hands of the hewers-but-not-partakers of black gold by divine zoning. Even then it was given unto me in a dream yesterday to rise up and go to the city of the usurper and reclaim the throne of our fathers. I have summoned thee here to bless my Al-Isra."

And there was great rejoicing among the princes of the tribe of cattle rearers. And Badamasi, whose shekels still overfloweth from the proceeds of his first eight years on the throne of his fathers, brought forth musicians who played the horn, flute, zither, lyre, harp and all kinds of music. And as the music roared, Badamasi bade his servants: "Bring forth the best robes and put it on my guests; and put rings on their hands and shoes on their feet; and bring hither the fatted calf and kill it; and let us eat and drink and be merry. For the throne of my fathers was lost and shall be found again in the year of the lord two thousand and eleven."

And while he tasted the wine, Badamasi commanded his servants to bring the golden and silver vessels which he had taken out of the palace when he ruleth over the land so that he and his lords and his wives and his concubines might drink therefrom. They drank wine and praised the gods of gold, and of silver, of brass, of iron, of wood, and of stone.

And in the same hour of their feast came forth the fingers of a man's hand and wrote over the candlestick upon the plaster of the wall of Badamasi's banquet room. And Badamasi saw the part of the hand that wrote and his countenance changed and his thoughts troubled him. And the joints of his loins were loosed, and his knees smote one against the other.

And Badamasi cried aloud to bring in the scribes and knowers of every manner of papyrus from west to east and from the middle to the deep South of the land, for his own tribesmen showeth interest only in one great papyrus from the land of Arabia and loathed every other manner of papyrus from the rest of the earth. And his servants went to the land of the merrymakers in the west and the land of the black Jews in the east and the land of the hewers-but-not-partakers-of-black-gold in the deep South and sought out the great knowers of every manner of papyrus amongst them.

And when the servants hath questioned the wise men assembled, two found favour and were brought before Badamasi. And Badamasi spake and saith unto the two wise men: "Whosoever shall read this writing and show me the interpretation thereof shall be clothed with purple and have a chain of gold about his neck and shall be the third ruler in the kingdom when I regain my lost throne." The first wise man was called Chidilech whose father was Amutalem the sower; the second was called Omoruch who came from the loins of Omoruyim the Edomite.

And it came to pass that Chidilech and Omoruch could not read the writing nor make known to Badamasi the interpretation. And

Chidilech the son of Amutalem the sower threw himself on the ground and saith: "My lord and master, though I know not the interpretation of this writing, I testify that thou art the prince of the Nile and thine goodness endureth forever. I assure thee, my lord and master, that a thousand shall fall beside thee, and ten thousand at thine right hand but it shall not come nigh thee. Only with thine eyes shall ye behold and see the reward of thine wicked enemies. Ride on in glory, my master, and reclaim the throne of thine fathers." And Omoruch the son of Omoruyim the Edomite also did obeissance and saith: "Forgive me, my lord and master, for age is come upon me and I no longer know the ways of the papyrus like the years of yore when I was but a humble servant in thine palace."

Whereupon Badamasi was greatly troubled and his countenance was changed in him and his servants were perplexed. And it came to pass that some of the servants came to Badamasi and saith: "Master, let not thy thoughts trouble thee nor let thy countenance be changed. There is a scribe called Ganimacchus from the town of Lokilius in the province of the merrymakers in whom is the spirit of the holy writs; and light and understanding and wisdom, like the wisdom of the gods, are found in him; and he spake truth to power without fear and he was made master of the scribes and knowers of papyrus. Even the Pharisees and the Sadducees found in him an excellent spirit full of knowledge and understanding. Interpreting of dreams and showing of dark sentences and dissolving of doubts were found in the same him. Now let Ganimacchus be called and he will show the interpretation."

Then was Ganimacchus brought in before Badamasi who spake and saith: "Art thou Ganimacchus who art from the town of Lokilius in the province of the merrymakers of the west? I have heard of thee that the spirit of the gods is in thee and that light and understanding and excellent wisdom are found in thee. I have heard that thou art fair and fearless. And now the wise men and the enchanters have been brought in before me that they should read this writing and make known unto me the interpretation thereof. But they could not show the interpretation of the thing. But I have heard of thee that thou canst give interpretations and dissolve doubts. Now, if thou canst read the writing and make known to me the interpretation thereof, thou shalt be clothed with purple and have a chain of gold about thine neck and shalt be the third ruler in the kingdom when I regain my throne."

Then Ganimacchus answered and saith unto Badamasi: "Let thy gifts be to thyself and give thy rewards to another, for I do not partake of the feast of rulers; nevertheless I will read the writing unto thee and make known to thee the interpretation. It was given unto thee, O Badamasi, to rule over this land for eight years but thou hast not humbled thine heart. The corruption of thine ways brought pestilence and the abomination of desolation upon this land. Thou ruineth even thine own tribe during thine reign."

And Ganimacchus added: "Now thou seekest to regain thine throne of yore and reclaim thine kingdom. Then I AM THAT I AM, the fiery one who answereth by fire and visiteth the iniquities of fathers upon their sons even unto the third and the fourth generations, sent this hand to write on the wall and condemn thee for thou hast sinned and come short of His glory. And this is the writing that was inscribed on your wall, O Badamasi. MENE, MENE, TEKEL, UPHARSIN."

Whereupon this interpretation came forth from the mouth of Ganimacchus: "MENE – God numbered thine kingdom and brought it to an end in the year of our lord one thousand nine hundred and ninety-three; TEKEL— thou art weighed in the balances and found wanting by God and the people of this land; PERES – thy kingdom is divided and given now unto the hewers-but-not-partakers-of-black-gold from the deep South that they may partake for the first time in their lives of the fruit and the increase of their own soil and, after them, it shall be given unto the black Jews of the east for thou hast refused to divide the yellow sun into two and grant them half of it since the end of the great war."

And it came to pass that Badamasi was greatly troubled by these revelations, whereupon he rent his clothes and ate nothing for seven days and seven nights. And when the sun had shewn its face on the eighth day, Badamasi summoned his servants and viziers and saith: "Lo,

I promised the people of my tribe to go forth on Al-Isra and reclaim my throne that was usurped many years ago. But seeing the interpretation of the writing on the wall that was shown me by Ganimacchus of the town of Lokilius whom you brought before me, go ye forth now and tell the people of my tribe that I no longer seek the throne of my fathers."

And the servants and viziers threw themselves on the ground and saith: "O Badamasi, we shall do thine bidding. But, pray, give us a reason. What shall we tell thine people?" Whereupon Badamasi saith unto them: "You shall tell my people that Sambo the Kadunite who now works for the usurper as the second ruler of this land is from the loins of the son of the nephew of my grandfather's uncle. Sambo the Kadunite is therefore a junior brother and son unto me. He is the flesh of my flesh and the bone of my bones. Seeing that he is now part of the throne of the usurper from the land of the hewers-but-not-partakers of black gold, I do not wish to covet my brother's property. So let it be written, so let it be done."

The Eighth Seal

(June 2010)

And I saw the angel with the eighth seal who smiled and said to me: "Paul, because you have heeded the principles of your calling and named your church in Lagos, House on the Rock, as I instructed you to do when I lifted you out of the doldrums in the United States and returned you to Nigeria, it shall now be revealed unto you what fate the angel with the seventh seal has reserved for Nigeria. For that country has sinned and come short of the glory of God." And I asked of the angel in total humility and submission of the spirit: "Pray, what ominous fate does the bearer of the seventh seal have for my country and how may I know and save the Chosen?"

And the angel with the eighth seal did *amebo* on the angel with the seventh seal. Thus it was revealed to me that the angel with the seventh seal had seven trumpets, and seven bowls with contents destined for Nigeria because of the iniquities of the land. And it was given to me in spirit to listen to the sound of the trumpets and it was worse than the heinous buzz of the vuvuzelas of Chaka's kraal. And the angel with the eighth seal ministered the meaning of the seven trumpets and seven bowls unto me.

And I was told that at the sound of the first trumpet, a mixture of hail and fire shall come over Nigeria such as the earth hath never witnessed before; at the second trumpet, all the mountains in Nigeria shall be hurled into the sea and a third of all living creatures shall die; at the third trumpet, a blazing star shall fall from the sky into the rivers

Niger and Benue and the waters therefrom shall turn bitter; at the fourth trumpet, a third of the moon and the sun and the stars shall be struck and darkness shall come over the land; at the fifth trumpet shall begin the first real woe for the great Abyss shall open to let out smoke, locusts, snakes and scorpions and they shall be given the power to bite and torture 140 million people but not kill them; at the sixth trumpet shall come the second woe for four angels shall lead an army of two hundred million on horses to invade your land. The heads of the horses shall resemble lions' and out of their mouths shall come fire, smoke and sulfur.

And I asked about the bowls, for great fear and trepidation came upon me. And I was told that the seventh trumpet, which is the third woe, shall also release the seven bowls. The content of each bowl shall be poured on the land of Nigeria. The content of each bowl was shown to me but they are too fearful to be named. They are worse than all the calamities and the pestilence of the trumpets as I have already revealed them. They come with tsunamis, peals of thunder and earthquakes to be visited on Nigeria.

And I asked: Who shall I save from this revelation? How shall I save them? How shall I know the sign? And the angel with the eighth seal said to me: "Of all the thieves that are scattered over the face of the earth, the thieves in charge of your country have found favour with the Most High. They loot billions but they remember to render unto Caesar what is Caesar's and unto God what is God's. They take a high percentage of their loot to the Lagos-Ibadan expressway every Sabbath day. The make God the alpha and omega of everything they do with, and to, Nigeria. And because they are God-fearing thieves, prosperity pastors have been called to their service that they may not worship in the company of the wretched of the earth. Those are the people that you shall save from the fury of the angel with the seventh seal. For it is written that unto those who have, more shall be given. The little that belongs to the wretched of your country shall be taken from them and added unto the increase of the thieves.

At this point, I removed the sandals from my feet for I knew that I was in the presence of the Lord. And I asked the angel with the eighth seal: "How shall I make this rich and mighty people worship in comfort, away from the filth of wretched Nigerians?" And the angel said to me: "It was written in Nehemiah 2:20 that 'the God of heaven will give us success; therefore we His servants will arise and build.' Paul, my son, you and Ifeanyi must rise now and build a temple in Lekki of such luxury and splendour as has not been seen since the Temple of Solomon. You must call it The Millennium Temple. The air conditioning at The Millennium Temple must be worth ₦410 million and you must buy it from China. People will behold the temple you shall build and every tongue shall confess that the Lord is God."

And I asked the angel: "Where shall I house these people? Where shall they worship in luxury and comfort until the Temple is built?" And the angel said to me: "Paul, rise up now and rent the Eko Expo Centre at the Eko Hotel and Suites, Victoria Island, Lagos. The luxurious hall goes for N8.5 million a day and you must rent it for a minimum of two days. There, your congregation shall worship and give praise unto the Lord. After two days in Lagos, you shall charter planes and fly them all to New York and rent a hall in the Waldorf Astoria. You and your congregation must remain in New York and worship at the Waldorf Astoria until you complete The Millenium Temple in Lekki."

And I asked the angel: "Only less than one per cent of the population of Nigeria fall within the stratospherically wealthy bracket of my clientele. What shall I tell the more than 140 million of them who are indigent and will complain about the assignment you have given me?" And the angel with the eighth seal said to me: "Their complaint is already at hand. For tomorrow a newspaper called *P.M. News* shall carry a screaming headline— "Church Shells Out ₦17m To Rent Hall." The news that Pastor Paul Adefarasin and his wife spent seventeen million naira just to fellowship in luxury for two days will spread like a virus in cyber-Nigeria. From the Nigeria Village Square to Sahara Reporters, from Nairaland to Naijapolitics, there shall be cries of anguish and indignation from shocked Nigerians. They will abuse you and call you names for displaying such eye-popping ostentation in a land of bone-wracking poverty. That is what they did to my anointed, Daddy G.O, when he bought his private jet."

And I implored the angel with the eight seal to teach me how to respond to allegations of insensitivity. And the angel laughed and said: "Paul, my son, you shall say nothing. For when Nigeria's army of poverty rose against my anointed for buying a private jet, Jehovah the God of Abraham and Moses raised the mighty pen of Dele Momodu to come to the defense of the Chosen One. And Dele Momodu wrote to remind Nigeria's army of poverty that their brains are so dulled and corroded by poverty that a private jet bought with chicken feed, something that small boys in Hollywood play with, appears a big deal to them. Even so will I cause the same Dele Momodu to be distracted from his presidential campaign. And he shall rise and chastise Nigeria's 140 million army of poverty for complaining that you spent ordinary seventeen million naira to rent a fellowship hall for two days. For it is written that heaven and earth shall pass away but not a word of the eighth seal as has now been revealed to you shall pass away."

And I woke up from my trance. Hello somebody!

Hi Pastor!

The good Lord is good!

All the time!

The Prodigal Son

(July 2010)

In the fiftieth year of the slavery of the tribe of the owners-but-not-partakers of black gold in the deep South, God gave ear to their cries and hearkened. And there was a man named Jona the Teacher who was of the House of Fedora. And God came upon Jona in a dream and saith: "Lo, I have seen the affliction of your people whose black gold hath been stolen these past fifty years to build other peoples' tents; I have heard their cries on account of their taskmasters from the desert. Indeed, I know their sufferings and I have come down to deliver them from bondage and to place on their tongues the milk and honey that floweth out of the abundance of their land for the first time in their lives. So, come, I will send you to the city of the Rock in the land of the taskmasters of the desert and place you on the great throne from whence cometh all power."

And Jona fell on his face and saith: "My Lord and my God. Be it done to me according to thine will." And the word of the Lord came to pass and Jona the Teacher was indeed placed on the throne of power after death hath looked upon King Yaru of the tribe of the desert taskmasters who had gone to seek healing from the descendants of Ishmael. And there was great rejoicing among the tribe of the owners-but-not-partakers of black gold in the deep South for the hour of their redemption is indeed come. And they lifted up their eyes unto the mountains and sang:

We have overcome
We have overcome
We have overcome today
Oh deep in our hearts
We do believe
We have overcome today

And their leader, a fiery patriarch called Clarkodemus, saith unto the desert taskmasters of yore: "Touch not Jona my anointed, for who God hath blessed no man can curse!" And after the new King Jona had burnt a thousand offerings, the Lord appeared to him in a dream and saith: "Because thou hast found favour in mine eyes and art now king, ask whatever you want and it shall be granted unto thee."

And King Jona did obeisance and saith: "My Lord and my God, great indeed is thy faithfulness. You have been kind to me your servant by making me king and to my people in the deep South by giving us dominion over the black gold of our earth that was taken away for fifty years by our taskmasters from the desert. Therefore, I would have asked of thee wisdom and a discerning heart to rule over this 150 million people; I would have asked of thee knowledge to distinguish between right and wrong but, unfortunately, King Solomon already asked for all these things so many years ago before me.

"My lord and my God, being my own man, I do not want to copy the requests of King Solomon. Seeing that my people in the deep South have suffered and never made merry in fifty years, I ask that you grant unto me 16.4 billion shekels of our inheritance from the black gold that I may bring forth musicians to play the horn, flute, zither, lyre, harp and all kinds of music. King Solomon asked for wisdom. As for me and my household, we have decided to make merry."

And the Lord saith unto Jona the King: "Thou seeketh 16.4 billion shekels of thine inheritance to make music?" And Jona the King replied: "We shall also buy the best robes for our guests and we shall put rings on their hands and shoes on their feet. But if the size of my request meets with thine anger, pray, render unto me 10 billion shekels of my inheritance to make merry."

And the Lord saith unto Jona the King: "Thou seeketh 10 billion shekels of thine inheritance to make music and to buy robes and rings and shoes for thine guests?" And Jona the king saith unto the Lord: "We shall also kill the fatted calf and buy the best wine from the land of Cana. But I see wisdom in spending my inheritance carefully. Therefore, render unto me only 9.5 billion shekels that I may make merry." But the Lord again saith unto him: "Thou seeketh 9.5 billion shekels of thine inheritance to make merry?"

Whereupon King Jona's heart hardened. Foolishness and pride took dominion over his mind. And he saith unto the Lord: "I cannot go lower. Pray, grant me 9.5 billion shekels of my inheritance for I must not tarry to merry. For unto everything is appointed a time, a time to dance and a time to drink." And the Lord granted King Jona his wish. And there was great rejoicing among King Jona's servants. And a palace servant named Orontolum the Earth Warrior opened his mouth and saith unto the people: "Hear ye, hear ye, our dear King Jona is a listening King. For he has given ear to the voice of the people and we shall now make merry with only 9.5 billion shekels of our inheritance."

And they made merry.

And nights passed. And mornings came. And life got worse for the tribe of the owners-but-not-partakers-of-black-gold in the deep South even with their son as king; and nothing changed for the other people all over the rest of the land. And when a great famine and pestilence came upon the land, the people became agitated and cried up to the Lord: "Give us another king."

And King Jona rent his clothes and cried: "Lo, I have sinned against God and man. For I have squandered my inheritance on wine and music. Now pestilence and the abomination of desolation is come upon the land. I shall rise up now and go back to the Lord and say: 'Father, I have come back home to you. Naked I stand before you, a prodigal, like that great bard of the east before the watery presence of his Idoto. I am not worthy to be called your servant, let alone your son.

Pray, grant me but a second chance and I shall make right that which I made wrong.'"

And He who answereth by fire and visits the iniquities of wayward fathers upon their sons summoned his angels and saith: "Take this unworthy Jona away from my sight and cast him into the belly of the biggest whale in the deepest part of the Dead Sea and seal the mouth of the whale this time. For it was given unto this foolish man to choose wisdom and discernment to rule over 150 million people but he asked to make merry instead. It is meet that I condemn him like I condemned he who spared King Agag when opportunity was bestowed on him. For Jona was found but asked to be lost; he was given life but he asked for death. So let it be written, so let it be done."

And it Came to Pass!

(July 2010)

And it came to pass that on the 29th day of the fifth month of the year 2011, the people of the land of Sodom placed their backs on the ground and spread their two legs so wide apart that each leg reacheth unto opposite ends of the earth. And Moloch Yaddie and his children looketh unto and into the wide open vagina that has been given unto them to rape for another four years, and there was great merriment and rejoicing and they got drunk on the good wine they had looted from the land of Cana. And when the foams of wine cleared from their eyes, it came to pass that Moloch Yaddie and his children built a mighty altar to Beelzebub, their munificent god and inspiration, slaughtered all the cattle from the place from whence cometh the groundnut pyramids of the past, and gave thanks and praises to Beelzebub.

And it came to pass that Moloch Yaddie and his children made other demands of Beelzebub saying: "Oh ye Beelzebub our god and maker, to you be the glory for keeping this vagina that our fathers started raping on the first day of the tenth month of the year 1960 in the family. Make it come to pass that we shall also hand it over to our children and children's children as it was handed over to us. And please, Beelzebub, keep it as fresh and hairy as it has always been for we eat only bearded meat. Oh Beelzebub, if ye shall grant our request for another sixty years, we shall raise a mighty golden temple unto you such as the world has never seen. We have twenty million black and useless sheep disturbing our black gold. We shall slaughter them all in sacrifice to thee if ye shall but grant our humble request."

And it came to pass that Beelzebub looked with kindness upon the supplicants and made them promises, but with only one demand of his own. Beelzebub said unto his children: "Seeing that you are the Chosen in whom I am well pleased; seeing that you and your fathers hath maketh me happy since you took delivery of that land on the first day of the tenth month of the year 1960, be it not assigned unto you the task of building me a mighty golden temple for a golden temple I need not. Give unto me only the necks and blood of the twenty million black sheep blocking your black gold. Will you do that for me?" And it came to pass that there was even more rejoicing in the household of Moloch Yaddie. For it was cheaper to dispense with twenty million sheep than waste resources on building a mighty golden temple. And Moloch Yaddie replied: "Oh ye Beelzebub our maker, even as I kneel here in supplication before thee, I have already ordered that the necks and blood of the sheep of Gbaramatu land be brought unto thee as first instalment so that thou knowest that I, your worshipper-in-chief, am a man of my words."

And it came to pass that Beelzebub looked at the handiwork of Moloch Yaddie in Gbaramatu land and it was good. And Beelzebub said unto Moloch Yaddie: "Seeing the thoroughness of thine labour in the vineyard of blood in Gbaramatu land, be it granted unto thee and thine household one more request." And it came to pass that Moloch Yaddie went into counsel. What shall we ask of Beelzebub? What shall we ask? What shall we ask? More black gold? The heads of our enemies? The necks of our unpatriotic children who abuse us from abroad? More vaginas to rape? What shall we ask of Beelzebub?

And it came to pass that a man called Iborilech, the son of Ahimelech the Jebusite, found favour in the eyes of Moloch Yaddie. And Iborilech came unto Moloch Yaddie, did obeisance, and said: "Oh great Moloch, did the son of that carpenter from Nazareth not ask his followers to come and find rest? He said unto them: Come unto me all ye that labour and are heavy laden and I will give you rest. For my yoke is easy and my burden is light." And Moloch Yaddie nodded in agreement. And Iborilech continued: "Oh Moloch, let us ask the opposite of Beelzebub. The only burden and yoke we carry in your household, oh Moloch Yaddie, is the burden of Ghana-must-go bags. That is the burden that that foster son of a carpenter wants to make light! That is treasonable felony, oh Moloch. Who wants to carry lighter Ghana-must-go bags? How can a bag filled with dollars, pounds and euros be light? Ask of Beelzebub to make our burden and yoke even heavier."

And it came to pass that there was great rejoicing over the Solomonic wisdom of Iborilech, son of Ahimelech the Jebusite. And Moloch Yaddie said unto Iborilech: "Verily, verily, I say unto thee, today you will be with me in my Paradise on the Rock." And it came to pass that Beelzebub granted unto Moloch Yaddie and his children their request of a heavier yoke.

And their Ghana-must-go burden got heavier every day. And unto Iborilech was added forty billion of the heaviest Ghana-must-go burdens that Moloch Yaddie could find.

And it came to pass that Beelzebub got drunk on the praises and offerings he got daily from Moloch Yaddie and Iborilech. And it came to pass that Beelzebub overlooked Joseph the Carpenter, foster father of the man with the light burden, and mocked the Man's real Father saying: "Thou callest thineself 'I Am That I Am'. Thou maketh this land which thou namest 'Eden'. See as my children, Moloch Yaddie and Iborilech, overuneth and renameth it Sodom!"

And it came to pass that I Am got very angry at the effrontery of Beelzebub and vowed to destroy Beelzebub, Moloch Yaddie, Iborilech, and all the other demons who conquered Eden and renamed it Sodom. And it came to pass that the foster son of the Nazarene carpenter interceded with his real Father on behalf of Beelzebub, Moloch Yaddie, and Iborilech son of Ahimelech the Jebusite. "Father, do not destroy them. The Sodomites deserve them." And I Am That I Am asked: "Son, why speaketh thou thus?" And the son answered: "Father, thou maketh those Sodomites after our image but they cast away our image and taketh images we did not create. Thou giveth them the example of Ukraine and Iran, Ghana and Botswana, but they have eyes and do not see; they have ears but they hear not. Year after year, decade after decade, they lie flat on their backs, open their legs wide for Beelzebub, Moloch Yaddie and Iborilech. Father, thou hast never helped any people who did not first help themselves."

And it came to pass that I Am That I Am thought about the counsel of His son and it found favour in His ears. And it came to pass that on the weekly appointed day of Sabbath, the Sodomites rose, dusted their backs and buttocks, went to their places of worship, screamed unto I Am That I Am and His son: "Save us, please save us from Moloch Yaddie and Iborilech!" and returned immediately to their positions under Moloch Yaddie and Iborilech after the screaming.

King Jona's Legion

(August 2011)

And it came to pass that in the first year of the second period of King Jona's reign, a great torment came upon him and demons took dominion over his soul, even as pestilence and plagues ravaged the people of Sodom. And fear came upon his servants, for they knew not the source of their master's torment. And there was a new servant named Reuben the Scribe who hath written the king's praise ten times on ten scrolls before the cock crowed in order to be made a palace servant. And fearing for his new source of food and merriment, Reuben the Scribe summoned all the other palace servants, and saith: "Lo, it is true that I am new among thee. But seeing as our master is tormented by spirits and demons, it is meet that we send for healers from across the land."

And great sorrow is come upon the servants, for they hath no dominion over the spirits and the demons that tormented King Jona. The leader of the servants, a man named Orontolum, who was of the tribe of the drinking fishermen, saith unto Reuben the new servant: "It is meet indeed that we seek healers for our king, for all the shekels that we take from the people of Sodom and apportion unto our own inheritance cometh from the King. But seeing that thou art new here in the palace, thou knowest not that the palace hath no need of healers from this land, for there are better healers abroad. Only healers from other lands attend to the king and his servants."

And the other servants cried out in agreement with Orontolum the head servant. And a lad named Renokrim, whose task it was to show the naked King Jona's new and invisible clothes to the people of Sodom, cried louder than the other servants and saith: "O Orontolum our head servant, great indeed is thine wisdom for no native healer from the land of Sodom must touch our king. Be it known to Reuben the new servant that the king who reigned before King Jona sought healing from the great healers among the descendants of Ishmael in the land of Arabia. He did not seek healing from the native healers of the land of Sodom."

And Orontolum was pleased with the wisdom of Renokrim, for the boy hath a bright future as an unthinking slave of the throne. And King Jona's servants fanned across the face of the earth, looking for all manner of healers for their tormented master. And they sent emissaries to all the one hundred and twenty-seven provinces of the land of King Ahasuerus, who ruled from India to Ethiopia; and they went among the Hittites and the Amalekites; and they went among the Moabites and the Ammonites; and they went among the Jebusites and the Edomites; and they went among the Romans and the Corinthians; and they went among the Philippians and the Thessalonians; and they went among the Ephesians and the Galatians; and they went among the Gadarenes and the Nazarenes; but they found not a single healer who hath dominion over the spirits and the demons that tormented King Jona.

And it came to pass afterward that the Master of Ocean and Earth and Skies went from village to village making nature sweetly obey his will. And as he approached the city by the Rock from the desert lands to the north, a great sandstorm threatened him and his disciples. And the Master saith unto the sandstorm: "Peace, be still." And the sandstorm receded in obeisance. And the apostles were amazed. And when the sandstorm hath cleared, the Master of Ocean and Earth and Skies approached the city by the Rock with his disciples. And King Jona, who still hath found no healing for his torment and was now kept bound in chains and in fetters by Orontolum, Reuben and Renokrim, rushed out and fell down before the Master, and with a loud voice saith: "O Master of Ocean and Earth and Skies, what have I to do with thee? I beseech thee, torment me not."

And the Master spake directly to the demon inhabiting King Jona: "What is thy name?" And he said: "My name is Legion, for we are many demons that entered into the king." And the Master asked: "Who are the chief demons in the Legion?" And one saith: "I am the demon of greed and my name is Seven. I cause the king's heart to desire seven. Give him four shekels and he wants seven; give him four apples and he wants seven; tell him to know four women and he wants to know seven; give him four years and he wants seven." And another saith: "My name is Fiddle. When half his kingdom burns in the north, I make him desire to play with me; when floods consume his biggest city, I make him desire to play with me; when robbers maul his people, I make him desire to play with me; when the youth of his land hath no hope, I make him desire to play with me." And another saith: "My name is Exu. I gave him all his servants and advisers. I bought them all from the crossroads." One demon was named Hypnos. Another demon was named Bacchus. Thus did a colourful procession of demons come forth from King Jona's soul and declared their names to the Master of Ocean and Earth and Skies.

And because they were close to the north where there was no swine, for the natives followed the faith of the descendants of Ishmael and ate not unclean meat, the Master of Ocean and Earth and Skies thought of casting the demons into donkeys but his disciples came unto him and saith: "O Master of Ocean and Earth and Skies, thou healest ten lepers in Samaria but only one remembered to return and give thanks unto thee. We know not if this King Jona is like the nine ungrateful lepers. It is meet that you test him before you heal him."

And the Master was greatly pleased with his disciples. And he asked the tormented King Jona: "Thou desireth freedom from thine bondage to Legion?" And King Jona saith in a loud voice: "Please heal me, for my torment is great." And the Master saith: "Do you believe you can be healed?" And King Jona saith: "I believe, help my unbelief." And the Master saith: "If thou must be healed, go thy way, sell whatsoever thou hast, and give to the poor, and thou shalt have treasure in heaven and healing on earth. And come, take up the cross, and follow me."

And King Jona was sad at that saying and went away grieved for he had great possessions and hath plenty of shekels stolen from the people of Sodom; and he was blessed with a people who hath eyes but seeth not that he stole from them. And Reuben and Orontolom and Renokrim and all the other servants rent their garments and poured ashes on their own heads, in sorrow, for if King Jona obeyed the Master of Ocean and Earth and Skies and gave all his possessions to the poor, their own feasting on the inheritance of the people of Sodom would come to an end. And the Master looked at the grieving King Jona and saith to his disciples: "How hardly shall they that have riches enter into the kingdom of God!"

And the disciples were astonished at his words. But the Master answereth again and saith unto them: "Children, how hard is it for them that trust in riches to enter into the kingdom of God! King Jona and his servants preferred the shekels and the wine and the fatted calf that they steal daily from the people of Sodom to healing from the affliction of Legion. Verily verily I say unto thee, it is easier for a camel to go through the eye of a needle than for a rich man to enter into the kingdom of God. Therefore, let us shake off the dust of this land from our feet in testimony against King Jona and his servants, for none of them shall be with me in my Father's kingdom. So let it be written, so let it be done."

Balaam's Ass

(December 2011)

And it came to pass that after the people of Sodom hath shaken off the yoke of the taskmasters who ruleth over them in the name of the great white Queen in the land of the permanent rain, a long line of pestilential kings took dominion over them and visiteth upon them worse plagues than God hath visited on the people of Egypt during the reign of the Pharaohs.

And for fifty-one years, the kings of Sodom and their children's children sat on the back of the people of Sodom. And the new king, Jona, who was of the tribe of the fishers of fish, seeing that the back of the people of Sodom was sweeter than honey, summoned all the other kings who hath ruled before him and saith unto them: "Lo, it has been given unto me to sit on the back of the people of Sodom and rule over them. But seeing that thou all hast been here before me, pray, what must I do to inherit more years on the back of the people?"

And all the former kings were greatly pleased that the new king hath sought their wisdom and given them room to retire on the back of the people of Sodom even as they approached the evening of their own years. And Badamasi the Minnarite opened his mouth and saith: "Oh King Jona of the tribe of the fishers of fish, great indeed is thy wisdom for it has been given unto thee to reward the years we spent before thee on the back of this people. It is meet therefore that we call a great feast of kings such as the world hath never seen. And from the land of Aethiopia through the one hundred and twenty-seven provinces of the kingdom of King Ahasuerus even unto India, all the people of the world shall speak of the great feast of the kings of the land of Sodom. And when we hath finished the feast, the time shall be appointed to grant unto thee more years on the throne of Sodom and to make thee a fisher of shekels."

And all the old kings present were greatly pleased with the words of Badamasi the Minnarite, who spake for all of them. There was Aremus of the tribe of the merrymakers to the West unto whom it was given to rule the land of Sodom two times; there was Yak the Warrior who was sorrowful that the land of Sodom hath a great problem of too little knowledge about how to use so much shekel; there was Shehulem the Herdsman who saith yes unto every word uttered by his fellow kings; there was Shonekum, also of the tribe of the merrymakers, who sat only on one buttock on his seat near Shehulem the Herdsman; and there was Buharus, also of the tribe of the cattle rearers, who hath begun to dislike the ways of the old kings but still fellowshipped with them. And the old kings rejoiced and saith with one voice unto King Jona: "Give us a great feast on the back of the people of Sodom."

And King Jona's heart was gladdened by the disposition of the old kings even as there was great rejoicing among his palace servants. And King Jona summoned his servants who came into his presence doing obeisance. There was Orontolum the Earth Warrior who was also of the tribe of the fishers of fish; there was Reuben the Scribe unto whom it was once given to grieve for the people of Sodom who are heavy-laden; there was Renokrim, the lad who hath been brought into the palace by Orontolum to show the people the Emperor's new clothes; and there was Ken the Ogonite who grew in the shadow of a saint.

And King Jona saith unto his faithful servants: "Lo, I have summoned a great feast of all the old kings who sat on the back of the people of Sodom before me. Go ye now and bring forth musicians who play the horn, flute, zither, lyre, harp and all kinds of music. Bring forth the best robes and put it on my guests; and put rings on their hands and shoes on their feet; and bring hither the fatted calf and kill it; bring forth the best wine from the bridegroom's storage in the land of Cana;

and let us eat and drink and be merry. For it is appointed that after the great feast, the old kings shall grant unto me more years on the back of the people of Sodom and I shall add more food unto the portion of all my servants."

And great indeed was the feast of the new king and the old kings on the back of the people of Sodom. And while he tasted the wine, King Jona commanded Orontolum, Reuben, Renokrim and Ken to bring the golden and silver vessels so that he and his guests and their wives and their concubines might drink therefrom. And they drank wine and praised the gods of gold, and of silver, of brass, of iron, of wood, and of stone.

And it came to pass that even as King Jona and his servants and the old kings feasted and made merry, nights passed and mornings came but life got worse for the people of Sodom. And when a great famine and pestilence came upon the land, the people became agitated and cried up to the Lord: "Give us another king." But the Lord did not answer them. Whereupon the people sought counsel and saith: "For fifty-one years, we asked of our king's bread but they gave us stones; for fifty-one years, we asked of our kings fish but they gave us serpents. And now King Jona and his servants and all the old kings feast on our back even as great affliction is come upon us. It is meet therefore that we send for Balaam."

And it came to pass that the people of Sodom sent messengers unto Balaam the son of Beor to Pethor, which is by the river of the land of the children of his people, to call him, saying: "Behold, for fifty-one years our kings have given us plagues worse than the afflictions of the land of Egypt. And today, King Jona and all the old kings make merry on our back. Come now therefore, we pray thee, and curse King Jona and all the old kings; for they are too mighty for us. Peradventure we shall prevail, that we may smite King Jona and his servants and the old kings, and that we may drive them out of the land; for it is written that he whom thou blessest is blessed, and he whom thou cursest is cursed."

And Balaam went unto the Lord and saith: "The people of Sodom hath sent unto me, saying, Behold, our kings lay a heavy yoke upon us and they feast even as pestilence is come upon the land. Come now, curse me them; peradventure we shall be able to overcome them, and drive them out." And God said unto Balaam, "Thou shalt not go to Sodom; thou shalt not curse King Jona and the old kings." But Balaam rose in the morning, saddled his ass, and went in the direction of the land of Sodom.

And God's anger was kindled because he went. And the angel of the Lord stood in the way for an adversary against him. Now he was riding upon his ass, and his two servants were with him. And the ass saw the angel of the Lord standing in the way, and his sword drawn in his hand. And the ass turned aside out of the way, and went into the field. And Balaam smote the ass, to turn her into the way. But the angel of the Lord stood in a path of the vineyards, a wall being on this side, and a wall on that side. And when the ass saw the angel of the Lord, she thrust herself unto the wall, and crushed Balaam's foot against the wall. And he smote her again. And the angel of the Lord went further, and stood in a narrow place, where was no way to turn either to the right hand or to the left. And when the ass saw the angel of the Lord, she sat down under Balaam, and Balaam's anger was kindled, and he smote the ass with a staff. And the Lord opened the mouth of the ass, and she said unto Balaam, "What have I done unto thee, that thou hast smitten me these three times?"

And Balaam said unto the ass, "Because thou hast mocked me. I would there were a sword in mine hand, for now would I kill thee." And the ass said unto Balaam, "Am not I thine ass, upon which thou hast ridden ever since I was thine unto this day? Was I ever wont to do so unto thee?" And he said, "Nay." Then the Lord opened the eyes of Balaam, and he saw the angel of the Lord standing in the way, and his sword drawn in his hand. And he bowed down his head, and fell flat on his face.

And Balaam returned home and sent forth word to the people of Sodom, saying, "I shall not come to Sodom, neither shall I curse King Jona and thine old kings." And the people of Sodom were sorrowful and they lifted up their voices unto the Lord, saying, "Save us from the bondage of King Jona and the old kings for our pain is great!" Whereupon an angel of the Lord appeared unto the people of Sodom and saith: "True the Lord has seen your affliction; true the Lord has seen the iniquities of King Jona and his servants, but he has not granted leave unto Balaam to come and curse King Jona and your other kings for you." And the people wailed and saith unto the angel: "Why would the lLord keep us under the yoke of King Jona and the old kings? Why would the Lord not save us from the oppressor? Our torment is great."

And the angel saith unto them: "Lo, for fifty-one years the Lord hath given unto thee legs, hands, and voices to rise up against thine oppressors and say nay unto their ways; even Balaam's ass, which is but an animal, knew not to ask the Lord or foreigners to free it from the yoke of the oppressor. Behold, Balaam's ass knew the appointed moment to sit, move no more, and say no when the oppressor would ride it to certain death at the blade of my sword. Thus saith the Lord God of Israel to you people of Sodom: because Balaam's ass, an animal, has been wiser than thee who art people, it shall be appointed unto no foreigner to curse King Jona and the old kings for thee. Only with thine own hands must thou tear their flesh and feed them to the birds of the air; only with thine own legs must thou rise and kick against them; only with thine own voices must thou say nay like Balaam's ass. Thou must shake off the yoke of thine oppressors and curse them and their servants and their children's children. For I am the Lord your God and I will not do for thee that which an ass did for itself. My rod and my staff shall not comfort them who willingly spread their backs for iniquitous kings. So let it be written, so let it be done."

The Last Stone

(July 2012)

Vanity of vanities, saith the Preacher, vanity of vanities, all is vanity. But the people came upon the preacher and saith: If what thou sayest is true and all is indeed vanity, what sayest thou of King Jona, our taskmaster, and his wife? And the Preacher saith unto the people: Who is King Jona?

Whereupon the people spake about their tormentor and his wife and the abomination of desolation they hath wrought upon the land. And they saith: O preacher, thou knowest not King Jona and his wife? And they saith: Our ground and inheritance brought forth plentiful. But whilst we perish of hunger, King Jona and his wife apportioned our possessions unto themselves, unto their children, and unto their children's children. And when they hath filled their house with our portion, King Jona saith unto himself, "What shall I do, because I have no more room where to bestow my fruits?" And he saith, "This will I do: I will pull down my barns, and build greater; and there will I bestow all my fruits and my goods. And I will say to my soul: Soul, thou hast much goods laid up for many years; take thine ease, eat, drink, and be merry.'

After King Jona hath said these things, his wife's heart was greatly gladdened. And she summoned Orontolum, Renokrim, Abatimus, and all the other palace servants and saith: "Now that the inheritance of the people hath yielded plentiful for my husband's barns, it is meet that we call a great feast for all the lords of the land so we can rejoice and make merry. Go ye now and bring forth musicians who play the horn, flute, zither, lyre, harp and all kinds of music. Bring forth the best robes and put it on my guests; and put rings on their hands and shoes on their feet; and bring hither the fatted calf and kill it; bring forth the best wine from the bridegroom's store in the land of Cana; and let us eat and drink and be merry."

And as they made merry, one of the lords of the land rose and did obeisance to King Jona and his wife and saith: "O great king, because it is appointed unto thee to rule over this land forever and to fill thine barns with the fruits and goods of the people, it is meet that we name this district after thee and in thine honour." Whereupon King Jona saith: "O worthy servant, so let it be written, so let it be done." And the choice district of the city bore King Jona's name henceforth. And another servant rose and saith: "O king, it is meet that we also name a road after thine wife, our mother." Whereupon King Jona saith: "O worthy servant, so let it be written, so let it be done." And a choice road in the city bore the Queen's name henceforth.

And one of the lords, who came from the home district of King Jona, rose and did obeisance and saith: "O great King Jona, although thou now liveth in the city by the Rock with the Queen our mother, it is meet that I appoint her one of the supreme courtiers in our home district." And there was great rejoicing in the hearts of King Jona and his Queen at this announcement. And while they tasted wine, King Jona commanded his servants to bring the golden and silver vessels so that his lords and their wives and their concubines might drink therefrom. They drank wine and praised the gods of gold, and of silver, of brass, of iron, of wood, and of stone.

And the people saith unto the Preacher, behold King Jona has built bigger barns to store the fruit of the people which he hath apportioned unto himself; behold a district is named after him; behold a street is named after his wife; behold his wife is appointed a supreme courtier in their home district. Before our own eyes, King Jona and his wife store up great treasures on earth and no moth or rust is come upon them and thou sayest that all is vanity? Pray, preacher, where is the vanity?

And the Preacher went out and departed from the temple. And the people came to him and taketh him up into an exceeding high mountain, and sheweth him all the worldly treasures of King Jona and his Queen and the glory of them. And they saith to the preacher: "Behold, with our eyes and out of our poverty and deprivation we behold the glory and splendour of King Jona's barn. Pray, preacher, where is the vanity?"

And the Preacher saith unto them: "See ye not all these things? See ye not King's Jona's treasures which he took from the people and apportioned unto his own inheritance? See ye not his mighty castles and his barns full of the fruits of the people? See ye not the district named after him and the street named after his wife? Verily verily I say unto you, there shall not be left one stone upon another that shall not be thrown down when the appointed time comes. For all the fullness of King Jona's barns shall come to nought and the souls of the foolish who build bigger barns for their earthly fruits shall be required of them. And that which was named after them today shall be erased and named after their successors. For vanity of vanities, all is vanity."

And great fear is come upon the people, for they look into the Preacher's eyes and saw the truth.

King Jona's Miracle

(April 2013)

Reworked and extended version of The Prodigal Son (Page 100)

And it came to pass that on the fiftieth year of the slavery of the tribe of the owners-of-black-gold-but-hewers-of-stone in the deep South, God gave ear to their cries and hearkened. And there was a man named Jona the Teacher who was of the house of Fedora.

And God came upon Jona in a dream and saith: "Lo, I have seen the affliction of your people whose black gold hath been stolen these past fifty years to build other peoples' tents to the north of the river; I have heard the cries of your people on account of their taskmasters from the desert.

"Indeed, I know their sufferings and I have come down to deliver them from bondage and to place on their tongues the milk and honey that floweth out of the abundance of their land for the first time in their lives. So, come, I will send you to the city by the Rock in the land of the taskmasters of the desert and place you on the great throne from whence cometh all power."

And Jona fell on his face and saith: "My Lord and my God. Be it done to me according to thine will."

And the Word of the Lord came to pass and Jona the Teacher was indeed placed on the throne of power after death hath looked upon King Yarus of the tribe of the desert taskmasters who had gone to seek healing from the descendants of Ishmael in the land of Arabia.

And there was great rejoicing among the tribe of the owners-of-black-gold-but-hewers-of-stone in the deep South for the hour of their redemption is indeed come. And they lifted up their eyes unto the mountains and sang:

We have overcome
We have overcome
We have overcome today
Oh deep in our hearts
We do believe
We have overcome today

And their leader, a fiery patriarch called Clarkodemus, saith unto the desert taskmasters of yore: "Touch not Jona, my anointed, for who God hath blessed no man can curse!"

And after the new King Jona had burnt a thousand offerings, the Lord appeared to him in a dream and saith: "Because thou hast found favour in mine eyes and art now king, ask whatever you want and it shall be granted unto thee."

And King Jona did obeisance and saith: "My Lord and my God, great indeed is thy faithfulness. You have been kind to me, your servant, by making me king and to my people in the deep South by giving us dominion over the black gold of our earth that was taken away for fifty years by the taskmasters from the desert. Therefore, I would have asked of thee wisdom and a discerning heart to rule over this 160 million people; I would have asked of thee knowledge to distinguish between right and wrong but, unfortunately, King Solomon already asked for all these things so many years ago before me.

"My lord and my God, being my own man, I do not want to copy the requests of King Solomon. Seeing that my people in the deep South have suffered and never made merry in fifty years, I ask that you grant unto me, my wife, and the guardian-warriors of the black gold of my people the years of Methuselah whereupon we may live forever to make merry and recover the locust years we lost to our taskmasters from the north.

"Grant unto me the wisdom to make merry with the shekels that cometh out of the abundance of black gold in the land of my fathers. Let my mouth sayeth unto my servants: bring forth musicians to play the horn, flute, zither, lyre, harp and all kinds of music for that which was taken by our taskmasters in the north has been rendered unto us tenfold. King Solomon asked for wisdom. As for me and my household, we have decided to make merry."

And the Lord saith unto Jona the King: "Thou seeketh the shekels of thine inheritance to make merry?" And Jona the King replied: "We shall also buy the best robes for our guests and we shall put rings on their hands and shoes on their feet. We shall kill the fatted calf and buy the best wine from the bridegroom's store in the land of Cana. And we shall say unto our guests: Rejoice and be glad for that which was taken from us hath been restored."

And the Lord cast King Jona away from His presence. Whereupon King Jona's heart hardened. Foolishness and pride took dominion over his mind. And he sent forth for all the guardian-warriors of the black gold from the land of his fathers and saith: "Come thou now into the kingdom of this world and partake of the bounties which hath been added unto our inheritance. Thine bellies shall be the bellies of our people. Whatever thou eateth shall be considered eaten by our people."

And the guardian-warriors of black gold who hath lived by the sword and by blood in the creeks and the bushes made haste to the city by the Rock. One was called Tompolus the Mighty and the other was called Asarius the Ijawmite. And they came into King Jona's presence and did obeisance. Whereupon great joy is come unto King Jona's heart upon seeing his brothers.

And the king saith unto the guardian-warriors: "Brothers, I welcome thee into our inheritance. Look at this great city by the Rock, look northward and southward, look westward and eastward, all that you see was built with our black gold and upon our backs by our taskmasters of yore. Now eat and let us make merry for that which was taken from us hath been restored tenfold."

And there was great rejoicing among King Jona and his brothers from the creek, Asarius and Tompolus. And they invited the palace servants to partake of the great feast. One was Orontus and the other was Renokrim, also of the creeks. One was Dokupemus, a moneychanger who hath robbed people in the land of the farmers in the middlelands and the traders in the east before he found favor with King Jona as a trumpeter. The other was Reuben the Ogunite, a junior trumpeter to Dokupemus.

And when their bellies hath filled with food and wine, Dokupemus and Reuben cried forth and saith unto the assembly of King Jona and his brothers from the creek: "Though we come from the land of the merrymakers to the west, it is meet that we spit on the land of our forebears and adopt your land. The gods of your creeks shall be our gods and the ancestors of your creeks shall be our ancestors." And it pleased King Jona and Asarius and Tompolus what they heard from these two servants whereupon King Jona saith: "Dokupemus and Reuben, my humble servants, our gods shall be your gods and our ancestors shall be your ancestors."

And they made merry.

And nights passed. And mornings came. And life got worse for the tribe of the owners-of-black-gold-but-hewers-of-stone in the deep South even with their son as king; and nothing changed for the other people all over the rest of the land. And when a great famine and pestilence came upon the land, the people of the creeks became agitated and cried up to their son King Jona: "Give us bread and shekels."

And King Jona rent his clothes in anger and saith: "Lo, you people of the creeks, for three years now I have killed the fatted calf for our guardian-warriors, Tompolus and Asarius. Their bellies are your bellies. Whatever they eat into their own bellies is sufficient unto the people. I have given Tompolus dominion over the waters and unto Asarius I have given billions of shekels."

And nights passed. And mornings came. And the people of the creek were hungry still. And they came unto King Jona their son and saith: "Give us bread and shekels and water that we may wet our parched throats." Whereupon King Jona saith unto his people: "Lo, I still feed Tompolus and Asarius. Their bellies are thine bellies. When they feed, thou art fed. When they drink, thine thirst disappears. Go now in peace."

And nights passed. And mornings came. And the people of the creek were hungry still. But in the fourth year of King Jona's reign, he sent his servants forth into the creeks with a message for the people. And King Jona's servants went to the creeks and saith unto the people: "Lo, the time is come to choose a new King for the great throne of the land in the city by the Rock. Behold the evil taskmasters to the north, the greedy traders to east, and the lousy merrymakers to the west covet the throne of our son, King Jona. It is meet that we come together to secure the throne of our brother who hath fed two great bellies in the last four years. For he took our brothers Tompolus and Asarius out of the creeks and bushes and made moneychangers of them. And when they fed, the people fed, when they drank, the people drank, for their bellies are the people's belly. Let not our enemies to the east and to the west and to the north visit iniquities upon our inheritance."

And one poor fisherman who hath seen years and suffering rose and saith: "Lo, it is true indeed that our son hath been King in the last four years but, pray, how doth the food and the wine move from the bellies of Asarius and Tompolus into my belly? For I have known hunger in the last four years of King Jona, our son, like I knew hunger under our taskmasters from the north."

And great anger is come upon the servants of King Jona. Whereupon they called their centurions and saith: "Take this ungrateful fisherman and cast him into the lions' den. For he knoweth not that the hunger you suffereth in the hands of your son is sweeter than the hunger you suffereth in the hands of strangers.

"He knoweth not that the thirst inflicted on you by your brother is sweeter than the thirst inflicted by strangers. He knoweth not that when two of us eat, like brothers Tompolus and Asarius are eating from the table of our great King Jona, even so the multitudes are automatically fed, for their stomachs are the stomachs of the people.

"Cast this fisherman away and let it be said that though the Nazarene son of a carpenter fed the multitude with five loaves of bread and two fish, our King Jona hath performed a greater miracle these past four years for he fed only two bellies and the whole creek was fed. So let it be written, so let it be done."

Part Three:

Open Letters to Godot

Ambassador Ahmadu Alli Writes President Yar'Adua

(April 2008)

Dear President Yar'Adua,

Ranka dede, sir. *Saanu da aiki,* sir. I hope this letter finds you well. If so, doxology. I am constrained to write urgently to intimate you on the frustrating conditions I've had to contend with since I assumed duties as Nigeria's High Commissioner to the Republic of South Africa. You will recall, sir, that I had serious misgivings about being posted to this place but you reassured me that things would work out *insha Allah.* I must regretfully inform you, sir, that you were wrong. This place is hell and I don't know what I am doing here. The ways of the South Africans are indeed very strange.

The first serious signals of South Africa's backwardness and dysfunctionality became apparent when I landed at the airport in Johannesburg. I was profoundly shocked to discover that only two official vehicles from the Nigerian embassy and three embassy staff were on hand to receive me. This was a serious breach of protocol. When was the last time I moved in anything less than a motorcade of twenty-five cars, heralded by AK-47-wielding soldiers and koboko-swishing mobile policemen sweeping civilians out of my way? I felt naked, empty and vulnerable. I felt betrayed by those embassy boys who appeared to have forgotten how we handle matters of protocol for people of my standing in Nigeria. Obviously, I wasn't going to subject myself to the indignity of leaving the airport in a "motorcade" of two miserable embassy vehicles. I sat put and told the boys to organise. They finally found a solution by renting five cars from the AVIS car rental outlet to bring the tally of vehicles to seven.

Needless to say, your Excellency, I had to "manage" a convoy of only seven cars. Without siren! As if this outrage wasn't enough, we had barely made it out of the airport when we found ourselves in one of Johannesburg's notorious traffic jams. Again, our boys from the embassy had no idea what to do. When we post these boys out, we must insist they visit Nigeria twice a year, your Excellency. They are completely out of touch. Just imagine, I had to suggest to them to phone the Chief of Army Staff and the Inspector General of Police to send troops to come and clear the road for us. Rather than act, they sat there looking at me with eyes so wide open they almost popped out of their sockets. Then one obsequious fool explained, "Things don't work that way here, sir." "How do you know, have you ever tried," I asked him.

I did not fare any better on my first day on the job, your Excellency. The first thing on my agenda was to present my letters of accreditation to President Thabo Mbeki. Regrettably, I left arrangements to our boys in the embassy. Their shoddy handling of the airport situation should have taught me a lesson! I had expected them to rent a white horse and a crowd of at least one hundred singing and drumming Nigerians to form a procession. I was going to ride the white horse through the streets of Pretoria, all the way to Union Building, with our people singing and drumming. You know, the way we do things back home. What did I get instead? The Ambassador's official car, a driver, and one miserable aide! At my urging, they had to rent five cars from AVIS! If I hadn't insisted, the boys would have done untold harm to Nigeria's image as the Giant of Africa by having her Ambassador drive to that ceremony in only one car. No policemen. No soldiers. No siren!

The humiliation continued when we got to Union Building. Only the official car with the Nigerian flag was allowed in. They wouldn't allow the rental cars in because they were not accredited. I told my aide to go and "see" the appropriate people only to be told by the rude boy that they don't "see" people in South Africa. How do you run a country where you don't "see" people? How do you get things done? Anyway, the ceremony went well, your Excellency. The only disappointing thing is the simplicity of the surroundings of President Mbeki. Things were so simple you had no idea you were in the Presidency. They are not doing Africa proud at all, sir. From what I saw, my estimation is that the budget that maintains the South African Presidency for a whole year is approximately the size of the weekly entertainment budget of a Nigerian Minister or Governor.

My second day on the job was even more frustrating, Mr. President. I was briefed that we had an application for a new plot of land languishing at the Pretoria City Hall. There is an embassy expansion project in the pipeline. Apparently, the application has been at City Hall for more than two years because the plot we want happens to be in a protected green area. My predecessors have had no luck with the Mayor. Pray, your Excellency, why deal with the Mayor when things could be accelerated the Nigerian way? So, I phoned the Mayor and respectfully and politely asked for the name and phone number of his Godfather. My intention was to "see" his Godfather and promise him an oil block allocation in the Niger Delta if he would prevail on his political godson to alter the Pretoria Master Plan and give us a plot in the green area. To my surprise, the Mayor told me that he had read Mario Puzo's novel but had never seen the movie! These South Africans are unbelievably backward! When I finally got him to understand what I meant, after almost an hour of explanation, he laughed condescendingly and said, "We don't do that in South Africa, Mr. Ambassador. We cannot alter the city's Master Plan." Unbelievable, isn't it? Have these people never heard of Abuja? So, what exactly do they do here? What is this idea of people getting elected to political office without Godfathers? I banged the phone on him. If I had continued the conversation, I couldn't put it past him to give me the extraordinary yarn that they also organise elections here without thugs, guns, and ballot box stuffing.

My nightmare in this country continued last week when I went to the University of Witwatersrand in Johannesburg. One of our very useful boys—an unemployed graduate of the University of Ibadan who helped organise the shipment of arms and recruited cult members to help us capture the Oyo State Government House for Alhaji Chief Alao Akala—has decided to quit the political scene in Nigeria and return to his studies. He emailed to notify me that he has an application for graduate studies at Wits. Could I please look into it? The boy served the PDP so diligently and I was inclined to help him. So I went to Wits last week to see the Registrar. She informed me that they did indeed receive the boy's application but he did not meet the minimum admission requirements for graduate studies at Wits. *Duh*, as if I didn't already know that before asking to meet with her! I asked if we could come to an agreement and opened the *Ghana-must-go* bag I had with me. Crisp bales of rand notes smiled from the bag. She screamed and sent me out of her office, claiming that she would have had me arrested if I didn't enjoy diplomatic immunity. As I did not want to return to Pretoria with the money, I made one last ditch effort. I phoned the University's information service and requested to speak with the Registrar's Garrison Commander. Predictably, nobody had any clue! I gave up on South Africa at this point. I mean, what kind of country is this? People get positions and appointments without Godfathers and Garrison Commanders. I don't understand. Your Excellency, there is really no place like home. All I would have had to do in Nigeria is place one phone call to any Vice Chancellor. The boy would end up in the Vice Chancellor's discretionary admission list with immediate effect.

Your Excellency, these unending insults and indignities are nothing compared to the stubbornness with which people address me here as Mr. Ambassador. Nonsense. I've insisted that they use the full list of my honorifics to no avail. Who would dare leave out anything from this list in Nigeria – Ambassador, Senator, Doctor, Chief Ahmadu Alli. Nobody here seems to understand that none of these items can be left out when addressing me. Mind you, to make things easy for the South Africans, I've even reluctantly left out all the items that would compulsorily come after my name in Nigeria – MON, OFR, GCFR, etc etc etc. Pray, if they can't get a paltry total of four honorific prefixes right, how are they going to contend with the suffixes?

Your Excellency, it is clear that I am not going to be able to stay here. I can't function. Their system is completely upside down. May I humbly request to be posted to Cameroon or Benin Republic? They are our neighbours. Years of associating with us have rubbed off on them. They know how things are done. They understand. If the slots in Yaoundé and Cotonou are not available, I won't mind the UK. The British are far more tolerant of the way we do things. They see no evil, hear no evil, and speak no evil in order not to endanger the oil flow. London is far more amenable to the Nigerian way than Pretoria. I should be able to function there.

Yours in service to Nigeria,
Ambassador, Senator, Doctor, Chief Ahmadu Alli, MON, OFR, GCFR, etc etc etc.

An Open Letter to Professor Ndi Okereke-Onyiuke, PhD, OON, Chairperson of TransCorp, etc

(August 2008)

Dear Professor Ndi Okereke-Onyiuke,

Greetings. I apologise for the cumbersome heading of this letter. I may be dangerously approaching one and a half decades in the West, but I am still very mindful of the importance of titles in Nigeria. I try to respect our sensibilities. I have also taken the liberty to address you as "Chairperson" as opposed to your normal designation as "Chairman" of TransCorp. You see, I live in North America and I don't want *wahala* with the feminists. But I digress. I am writing to congratulate you on the astounding success of your latest initiative and contribution to the advancement of the Black race – the launch, on Friday July 18, 2008, of the Africans for Obama 2008 Group. The launch was followed, last week, by a celebrity dinner/concert fundraiser for Brotha Barack's election project. It has now been widely reported that you were able to raise in excess of ₦100, 000,000 for the advancement of your worthy cause.

Prof, *shebi* you *kuku* know our people. I don't know about Nigerians in Nigeria but your venture has caused a combination of hurricane Katrina and Asian tsunami among diasporic Nigerians. They have invaded the internet in an unprecedented orgy of Ph.D – Pull Her Down. There is no name under the sun they have not thrown in your direction. They have gone fishing, and their hooks are pulling out all sorts of intents from the pond of speculation. Our people's capacity for *bad belle* is simply unbelievable. *Nne*, don't tell them that you heard it from me *o*, but some called you *419* and others called you an attention seeker. Some called you a saboteur out to create problems for a candidate who has to contend with rules that make it a felony for him to be admired by Europeans, let alone rowdy Africans in Lagos, Nigeria. The lawyers among them, sounding like characters in the court of Julius Caesar, have gone to town with their arcane legal Latinisms. They are debating things like the *locus standi* of your action; whether you have committed a crime *ab initio*; whether something else is going on *in loco delicti*; some are already planning to appear as *amici curiae* in case the Americans "catch you" and bring you to trial. Another category of *bad belle* Nigerians accuse you of outright immorality and unethical behaviour. They claim it is immoral and unethical for you to ignore all the problems of poverty in Nigeria and ship *Ghana-must-go* to the most affluent country on earth.

Fortunately, it is not all bad news, ma. You have found a very vociferous defender in a Washington-based Nigerian Professor who has considerable internet presence. He has been your rock of Gibraltar, a veritable Thomas, refusing to cast even one miserly stone until he has seen, heard, smelled, felt, and touched evidence of wrongdoing on your part. Like me, he believes that there is just no way a Nigerian "of timbre and calibre", like you, would be ignorant of financial regulations in American elections. I even went further. I told those who cared to listen that you most certainly needed money to cook and fortify Brotha Barack properly the African way. We all know he has too many enemies and he lives in a foolish society where African Insurance is looked down upon as primitive *juju* and backward superstition. Since Brotha Barack is unlikely to know what is good for him, in terms of the imperatives of African fortification, I guessed you had decided to do it for him by remote control. We all know that African *juju* no longer comes cheap, especially in Nigeria. In fact, I am surprised that Nigerian *juju* men are not yet quoted at the Nigerian Stock Exchange, when they now operate in billions and at Dow Jones proportions. After all, Ambassador Edem recently set the people of the Niger Delta back by one billion, two hundred and seventy five million naira to procure an African remote control that would enable him control the brains of the Bayelsa State Governor and the Vice President of Nigeria. Pray, if the ordinary heads of two thieving PDP politicians in Nigeria cost that much, does it not stand to reason that you would need double that amount to insure Brotha Obama's special head?

That was the line of defence I maintained until I finally got news today that you stated—in an eloquent opening speech at the fundraiser—that funds realised would be used to sponsor members of your Obama 2008 organisation to the Democratic Convention in Denver, Colorado. Apparently, your organisation wants Africans from Lagos to storm Denver in order to sensitise African Americans to their civic responsibilities. You are on a get-out-the-vote-for-Brotha-Barack mission. Shame on your detractors! They were all wrong. They thought you were going to "eat" the money!

Now that we all know what you plan to do with the money, those of us who supported and defended you and have now "earned the mouth to talk" must make recommendations. I don't know what your Ambassador and defender in Washington will recommend but I have a few suggestions. First, when members of your Obama organisation apply for American visas to attend the Denver convention, do not tell the American Embassy in Lagos that you are going to the Democratic National Convention in Denver. You will be denied entry visas on the ground that there is no such convention taking place in Denver. There is a Clinton Family Convention to which the Democratic Party and Barack Obama have been invited as sidekicks. Take note of that very important detail. The good news – President Clinton is the first "black" President of the US. He is a friend plenipotentiary of Blacks and Africans. Nothing would make him happier than to have a bunch of Nigerians from Lagos drumming and singing "winner o o o winner" at the convention venue. That would be great for President Clinton's black resume.

Your goal of coming to educate African Americans to vote for a member of the tribe is extremely important. There is always the possibility that African Americans have been afflicted by a particularly deleterious Nigerian virus that developed in the 1990s. Let me explain. One ugly development in the June 12, 1993 elections was that Hausa-Fulani people voted massively for Chief MKO Abiola and abandoned their own tribesman, Bashir Tofa. What kind of nonsense was that? Then came 1999 and the Yoruba disowned their own, Olusegun Obasanjo. How many Igbos voted for Chief Orji Uzor Kalu and Professor Pat Utomi in 2007? They even went about applying the one drop of blood rule in questioning Utomi's Igboness, as if it was Oduduwa that gave him the middle name Okedinachi. Now that Goodluck Jonathan is part of the furniture in Aso Rock, his tribesmen are the first to deride him as a houseboy. In essence, there is an ugly pattern of voting against the tribe in Nigeria, like so much hens pecking at the entrails of the offspring of fowls. Now, Nigeria is the Black world's largest non-nation. Any disease that afflicts Nigeria automatically afflicts the Black diaspora. You have thus correctly surmised that African Americans could very well have contracted that Nigerian disease and could vote against the tribe in November. This is what makes your humanitarian urge to educate them and prevent this looming disaster such a worthy cause.

I must warn you, though. There is a good number of African Americans who blame you and I entirely for slavery. They say the white slave buyer and hunter has no blame. They say the organizer of the Middle Passage has little or no blame. They say Massa of the Deep South has minimal blame. There exists a thriving industry of white exculpation. They say we were the greedy fools who sold them for bottles of cheap, bad, inferior rum. The grudge is five centuries old but it is still very much alive. Ever so often, there is an African American asking a continental African to apologise to him or her. Or asking: Why did you sell us? It has happened to me a few times in totally unexpected situations and I've had to give folks a piece of my vitriolic mind. There may be such career exculpators in Denver. They won't find it funny for a bunch of funny folks from the Heart of Darkness— who are responsible for slavery—to add insult to injury by lecturing them on voting and civic responsibility. Let's hope they don't notice that little oxymoron – Nigeria and responsible democracy. Be prepared.

Yours truly,
Pius Adesanmi.

An Open Letter to Mrs. Farida Waziri

(July 2009)

Dear Madam,

Fraternal greetings to you from the Elders Committee and the Chieftains and Stakeholders Caucus of the National Association of Nigerian Looters (NALUTA, for short). These are not the best of times for members of NALUTA, all respected elder statesmen and women and winners of various national honours. From Halliburton to Siemens, too many of our members have been needlessly embarrassed in recent times, what with their names and bank account details splashed all over the internet as well as in local and international media. In fact, but for President Yar'Adua's commendable sense of loyalty to his friends and authors of his landslide selection in the last presidential election, things would have taken an unsavoury turn for some of our most respected members. As if these embarrassments weren't enough, a new list of looters purportedly authored by you is now circulating on the internet.

Upon reception of that list, we at NALUTA set up a high-powered panel of inquiry into the immediate, intermediate and remote causes of the composition and release of that list by the EFCC. While the committee is doing its work, the General Assembly of NALUTA has mandated the Elders Committee and the Chieftains and Stakeholders Caucus to open up channels of fruitful dialogue with you in order to facilitate our collective quest to move Nigeria forward. A quick glance at your list reveals the inadvertent omission of three of the most devoted foundation members of our organisation: former President Olusegun Obasanjo, His Excellency Elder Chieftain Stakeholder James Ibori, and His Excellency Chieftain Stakeholder Bukola Saraki of the Societe Generale Bank fame. We humbly wish to state our opinion that you may have left out these three respected members of our association because you are under the impression that they alone made your appointment possible.

Madam Chairman Ma, we feel constrained to remind you that every member of NALUTA contributed in one way or the other to your selection, appointment and subsequent confirmation by the Senate. May we also categorically state that the composition and release of this list is in direct violation of the unwritten gentleman's agreement you reached with our Body Language Committee before we authorised Chieftains Ibori and Saraki to forward your name to Mr. President? We also cannot reconcile your latest move with the guarantees given us by our trusted friend, Barrister I-Don't-Care, the Honorable Attorney-General of the Federation and Minister of Justice. We believe you still remember why your predecessor, Nuhu Ribadu, had to go…

Madam Chairman Ma, in these times of global recession when even the world's richest people, from Bill Gates to Richard Branson, are watching their money and adopting various measures to cut spending, your list has exposed our members to undue pressure to spend and this is what most of our members find so unpardonable. We all know that Nigeria is a primitive rent society where members of the public expect people like us to eat the national cake and distribute the crumbs therefrom to the dregs of society through donations, charities, foundations and sundry people-oriented initiatives. This explains why communities fall over one another to give us chieftaincy titles, Universities scramble to award us honorary doctorates, organisations of every hue try to make us patrons. Every segment of society scrambles to make us chief launchers at their events.

In these times of recession, we cope with these demands by claiming to be broke. Only last week, one of our respected members donated only ₦100, 000 as chief launcher at a fund-raising ceremony for a proposed cottage hospital his home town. He told the happy villagers to “manage” the widow’s mite he donated because times are hard. Now, because of you and your list, those villagers know that he looted more than ₦10 billion. You have painted this elder statesman as a hypocrite and liar in the eyes of his people. One of our female members has a more embarrassing story. She had been approached by the parents of a desperate baby with a hole in the heart. The baby needed an urgent operation that would cost almost N5 million. She gave them a check of ₦20,000 naira, citing financial difficulty in these turbulent times. Now, your list says she stole millions! If the baby dies, what do you expect people to think of her?

You have also put us in a very tight spot with the Pentecostal industry. As we all know, the Pentecostal industry is the most vibrant sector of our economy, coming second only to the Oil sector. The endless fight between President Yar’Adua and his militants in the Niger Delta means that Pentecostalism is the only sector that is currently sustaining Nigeria’s economy. Madam Chairman Ma, you cannot claim to be unaware of the fact that the working relationship between NALUTA and the Lagos-Ibadan Express Way Pentecostal Development Association is central to the health of Nigeria’s economy. After all, you visited the Dean of this Pentecostal Association with every staff attached to your office. NALUTA’s relationship with Pentecostal leaders is based entirely on trust. We pay our tithe and make regular donations by declaring what it has pleased the Lord to add unto us and our inheritance.

Last week, one of our most respected members went to Daddy General Overseer to complain of financial trouble. He said he was so broke, his inheritance so depleted, that he could only donate ₦1,000,000 this time around to advance the work of God. Sensing that powers, principalities and dominions were at work to deplete the man’s inheritance and make poor bank accounts his portion, Daddy G.O. went to the Lord on his behalf. Only for your list to appear this week and put him in the bracket of those who stole between thirty to a hundred billion naira! You have disgraced this respected elder statesman. How is he now to look Daddy G.O. in the eyes? What kind of testimony do you expect him to give next Sunday? Already, members of the congregation's Disciplinary Committee are advising the poor man to sow ten percent of the total loot you announced as seed in the vineyard of the lord. That is the only way, they assure him, to redeem himself in the eyes of the Lord.

But that is not even the most troubling part of this unfortunate saga. Most of our members have been avoiding the Lagos-Ibadan Expressway churches since you published your list. All those churches now know what they have and no one really wants to be made to cough out ten percent of that money as seed. In essence, you may have irreparably damaged the long-standing and mutually-beneficial relationship between NALUTA and the nation's Pentecostal industry. At a time when President Yar'Adua considers Pentecostalism one of the critical sectors that could inch us closer to meeting the Millennium Development Goals, your action, Madam Chairman, amounts to economic sabotage.

Ma, you are giving disturbing signals. We know you are still one of us. We know you must appear to be doing something about corruption. We know you will ensure that cases against our members drag on and on and on. We know you will find favourable judges ready to sell slap-on-the-wrist judgments at a discount – we are grateful for your excellent handling of Chieftain Stakeholder Lucky Igbinedion's case. But we cannot be too sure. You see, Nuhu Ribadu fooled us. At first we thought his *gra-gra* was all appearances. By the time we realised that the foolish boy was indeed serious about fighting corruption, too much damage had been done. So we cannot take chances with you. Just to assure us that you are not gyrating towards the Nuhu Ribadu philosophy, would you be disposed to meeting with our Class Interests Assurance Committee at your convenience?

Warm Regards,
Elders Committee of NALUTA ,
Chieftains and Stakeholders Committee of NALUTA.

Cc:
President Yar'Adua.
Barrister I-Don't-Care.
Distinguished Senator David Mark.
Honourable Dimeji Bankole.
Chief Vincent Ogbulafor.
All PDP Governors.

God and Allah Write President Yar'Adua

(August 2009)

Dear President Umooru Yar'Adua,

I am directed to write you by the leadership of the Joint Consultative Assembly of Paradise, Hell, Al-Janna, and Jahannam – an oversight body put in place by the Grand Council of Angels and Malaikas mandated by God and Allah to supervise matters of accommodation and welfare for the human remittances we receive from earth. Apologies for using the name your predecessor called you during a famous telephone call. He used that name in the context of a grave matter of life and death. As the issue at hand is also a grave matter of life and death, I figure it is appropriate to use the name. As you no doubt have been briefed, Mr. President, the Federal Republic of Nigeria, under Generals Ibrahim Badamasi Babangida and Sani Abacha, signed a number of binding agreements with the Consultative Assembly to review the quota allotted to Nigeria under our Special Customers' Quota Expansion scheme. The scheme was designed to take care of the needs of customer nations with very generous yield in human remittances to each of our four accommodation zones: Paradise, Hell, Al-Janna, and Jahannam.

You will recall, President Yar'Adua, that world leaders too numerous to mention had benefited from this quota expansion scheme and sent people here without the risk of overstretching our accommodation facilities and welfare resources. The quota expansion scheme allowed us to take care of human remittances from Germany under Adolf Hitler, the Soviet Union under Josef Stalin, Cambodia under Pol Pot, Haiti under Papa and Baby Doc Duvalier, Zaire under Mobutu Sese Seko, South Africa under Henrik Verwoerd and Pieter Botha. We also accommodated the close to one million Tutsis sent here by the Rwandan genocidaires. In essence, we never had any problems with any member nation. Our system ran smoothly and efficiently until Nigeria happened to us.

When Nigeria's military rulers made a strong and persuasive case for the inclusion of your country as a beneficiary of our special quota scheme, we dusted our records and discovered that Nigeria, under General Yakubu Gowon, remitted a healthy figure in excess of two million souls between 1967 and 1970 – and that was the only reason your country's application was favourably considered in the first place. Nigeria's application for Gold Card customer status was thus approved. Little did we know at the time, Mr. President, that we had signed up a country that would become the most egregious abuser of our privileges and procedures since the formation of this organisation. I am sorry for the tone of this letter but I have been instructed to rein in Nigeria in unequivocal terms or expel her from the organisation altogether.

Our first and most serious problem with Nigeria has to do with your country's illegal use and abuse of facilities and resources not covered by the agreements you signed. Generals Babangida and Abacha signed Nigeria up for quota expansion under our Extremists, Enemies of the State, and Disgruntled Elements portfolios. This allowed us to take in the thousands of human remittances they sent to us as enemies of their respective regimes. Unfortunately, President Yar'Adua, none of these two former military rulers of your country was visionary enough to also subscribe Nigeria to our Needless and Preventable Deaths portfolio. Vision is a pre-requisite for leadership. Visionary leadership entails being able to determine, empirically and otherwise, the rate and magnitude of infrastructural neglect and collapse that would occur in Nigeria between 1985 and 2009 and sign up accordingly for the appropriate portfolio in our services.

Mr. President Sir, hundreds of thousands of your citizens have arrived here between 1985 and the current year 2009 as a result of avoidable or preventable road accidents linked to the condition of your roads; thousands arrive daily because of the condition of your hospitals. Mr. President Sir, this situation is made even worse by the fact that thousands of your citizens arrive here daily only to tell lies and all kinds of cock and bull stories, a detail that does not help your country's already poor reputation. They claim to have been sent here by fumes inhaled from generators! Can you imagine that, Mr. President? Because we are here in heaven, your citizens assume that we are cut off from current affairs on earth. As if we do not know that no country on earth would allow the embarrassment of letting a single citizen die from the inhalation of dangerous generator fumes in the 21st century!

What is even more baffling is that human remittances from places like Somalia, Darfur, and war-torn Congo do not arrive here telling lies about generator inhalation, meaning that they have electricity in those places. So, why are your people such pathological liars? They lie even when they don't have to. Imagine elderly people from Nigeria arriving here to spin yarns that they slumped while waiting in line to receive their pension and other retirement benefits. And they expect us to believe outrageous stories like that! Do we look like fools? Even Field Marshal Idi Amin Dada paid pension and retirement dues to elderly Ugandans. And who even queues up in front of a government office for such things in the 21st century? You check your bank account online and your pension is there as direct deposit when due. We simply don't understand why old people from Nigeria come here to tell lies about queuing up for pension and dying in the process.

Mr. President Sir, these human remittances from Nigeria in the category of Needless and Preventable Deaths have spiked to such an astronomical and alarming level since May 29, 2007 that the Consultative Assembly had to convene a special emergency session on Nigeria, the outcome of which is this letter. The point is that we no longer have the capacity or willingness to accommodate Nigerian human remittances in a portfolio for which your country has not signed up. Please find enclosed the relevant application forms, should your administration be willing to subscribe to the appropriate portfolio. Please note that

Nigeria will have to pay up a backlog of subscription and membership fees starting from August 27, 1985. Our investigations revealed that although budgetary allocations for Nigeria's membership fees have been made annually since 1985, your government officials have never made a single payment. We made several phone calls to your Ministry of Finance but were told every time that the Minister was "not on seat." We spoke to your Minister of Information but all she told us was that she would try and rebrand Nigeria's unpaid fees, whatever that means.

Permit me to state, Mr. President, that your administration's attempt to create equity and balance in the area of religion has not gone unnoticed here. For a very long time, the Nigerians who arrive here as a result of religious violence or your robust pacification programme in the Niger Delta area of your country have always been almost exclusively Christians, putting an enormous strain on our accommodation facilities in heaven and hell. We have had little or no remittances from Nigeria that we could accommodate in Al-Janna or Jahannam as the case may be. Our investigations revealed that this pattern is due to the fact that religious violence in the northern part of your country has almost always exclusively targeted southern Christians while your mop up operations in the Niger Delta also target predominantly Christian populations. We were therefore surprised to notice a spike in Moslem remittances in the past week. Some of the Moslem arrivals revealed, on interrogation, that the latest religious uprising in the northern part of your country was a Moslem against Moslem affair for the very first time. It was also gathered that as a result of this uprising, your administration applied, for the first time in the North, civilian pacification methods that Nigeria has reserved exclusively for the South since October 1, 1960, hence the spike in Moslem remittances.

Because we design our products to fit the profile of our existing or potential customers, I have been mandated to advertise some of our new products to you. After due consideration of the pattern of remittances from Nigeria, we have designed brand new Religious Violence, Militants Eradication, and Kidnappings portfolios that we believe your administration will find very attractive. I have included appropriate brochures and other advertisement material for consideration by your cabinet. If you subscribe to this new service, it will prevent us from dumping the Nigerians who arrive here under this new category in the Needless and Preventable Deaths portfolio as has been the case in the past. To encourage you to sign up for this portfolio, the first two thousand civilians to arrive here as a result of your administration's continuous pacification of the primitive tribes of the Niger Delta will be admitted free of charge.

I await a timely response to this letter from your administration.

Yours sincerely,

Signed: Clerk of the Joint Consultative Assembly of Angels and Malaikas
Cc: His Excellency Distinguished Senator David Mark, Senate President
His Excellency Honorable Dimeji Bankole, House Speaker
His Excellency Chief Michael Aondoakaa (SAN), Stenographer-General of the Federation.

An Open Letter to Abuja's Rats and Mosquitoes

(November 2009)

Dear Pests,

Barka da Sallah greetings to you in the name of Allah the Merciful and the Beneficent. It is with great surprise and sorrow that I have been compelled to write you this letter after reviewing President Yar'Adua's proposed budget allocations for the 2010 fiscal year. You are not unaware of the frosty relationship between the Lower and the Upper Chambers of the National Assembly. That impertinent small boy who heads the Lower Chamber does not know his mate. He has been poking his *boi-boi* fingers in my nose and competing for superiority with me. How old was he when I was Governor of Niger State? How old was he when I was Minister of Communication? He was probably in secondary school.

It is against this background of a small boy's scorn and *arifin* that I discovered that his own wing of the National Assembly was allocated the sum of one hundred million naira to get rid of rats and mosquitoes in the year 2010, whereas my own superior chamber was allocated nothing under that category. How can that small boy get a hundred million to clear rats and mosquitoes from one room, and I get nothing? Ordinarily, we get double of whatever they get, in our capacity as senior and superior lawmakers. Their one hundred million automatically entitles us to two hundred million—if not more—for the same pest eradication agenda.

The strange omission of the Senate from this vital allocation made me set up a high-powered commission of inquiry made up of fifty trusted, eminent and distinguished Senators. They were, among other things, to look into the immediate, intermediate, and remote causes of our exclusion from that allocation and to do a census of all rats and mosquitoes in the Senate as a basis for our making a powerful case for a supplementary budgetary allocation of two hundred million naira for pest eradication in the Senate Chamber for the year 2010.

Dear rats and mosquitoes, in the course of their patriotic and onerous assignment, members of the commission of inquiry were shocked that the census exercise on which we spent so much money yielded nothing. Absolutely nothing! We found not a single rat or mosquito in the Senate Chamber. Since the absence of members of your respective species from the Senate is about to cost us two hundred million naira, I had no choice but to set up another commission of inquiry to look into the immediate, intermediate, and remote causes of your unfortunate boycott of the Senate.

This second commission of inquiry made even more shocking discoveries. It would seem that all the rats and mosquitoes allocated by Mother Nature to the National Assembly Complex only go to the Lower Chamber. They practice some strange Apartheid policy that keeps the Senate out of the picture. Our rigorous investigations revealed that that small boy heading the Lower Chamber is behind it all. It was revealed to us that in anticipation of next year's budgetary allocations, he held secret meetings with the leadership of the rat and mosquito species in the Federal Capital Territory and bribed them to concentrate only on the Lower Chamber of the National Assembly. That devious move has now earned him and the pack he leads in the Lower Chamber a one hundred million naira windfall.

This explains why I am writing to ask you to reconsider your actions. You stand to benefit a lot more by working with me. For starters, would you be inclined to let me know how much he paid you to live exclusively in the Lower Chamber and procreate generously there? I am prepared to double or triple it and have your people migrate to the Senate if only to teach that boy a lesson. As you probably know, President Yar'Adua is in Saudi Arabia attending to his health. May Allah grant him quick recovery. His absence provides us with a window of opportunity to prepare a strong case for a supplementary budgetary allocation of two hundred million naira for pest and rodent eradication in the Senate.

If moral considerations make you a bit reluctant to violate the terms of your existing agreements with that small boy, there are other options. Since you rats and mosquitoes breed very rapidly and generously, you must have ample supplementary population in Abuja. How much will it cost us to rent a crowd of two thousand rats and two thousand mosquitoes to invade and infest the Senate Chamber for the next two weeks? Once we reach an agreement and you invade us, we shall invite friendly editors of friendly newspapers to come and see what is going on in the Senate. That would earn us screaming headlines such as: "RATS AND MOSQUITOES TAKE OVER SENATE"; "FORTY SENATORS HOSPITALISED FOR MALARIA."

With such friendly press, it would be easy for us to slot in the supplementary budget allocation request. It may seem funny that we are asking you to invade us in the Senate so that we can ask for money to fumigate the Senate Chamber and kill you in the process. Let me assure you that this is Nigeria. Not a single rat will be killed. Not a single mosquito will be killed. The fumigation will only take place on paper and it will be carried out by fictitious companies owned by... by... by... well, let's just say that your people will not die. Anyway, you probably already know this from your arrangement with our junior partners in the junior Chamber.

I await your response very eagerly. Time is of the essence.

Yours sincerely,
Distinguished Senator Chief David Mark,
Senate President,
Federal Republic of Nigeria.

Application Letter to Chief Bode George

(November 2009)

Your Excellency Chief Sir,

Fraternal greetings to you in the name of our Lord Jesus Christ. I hope this letter meets you well. There are so many things to say but I am just going to cut to the chase. Chief Sir, I do not want to be like those foolish Nigerians who fanned across beer parlours and paraga joints to celebrate your incarceration by one renegade Yoruba judge who behaved like a fowl with an appetite for the intestines of a hen. While the foolish Nigerians celebrating your temporary visit to Kirikiri—I don't believe you will spend two years—forget that they are concentrating on your today, I have wisely decided to invest in your tomorrow.

Chief Sir, I am saying in essence that I have decided to give my today for your tomorrow. As I am not a hypocrite like most Nigerians, Chief, I will *kuku* just tell you why I am interested in your tomorrow. It is not an empty tomorrow. It is one of the luckiest tomorrows I have ever encountered in my life. How many Nigerian tomorrows can boast of eighty billion naira? That is the tomorrow you will return to from Kirikiri. Eighty billion naira in mint—*aganran*—condition. You see, in all things, we must give thanks and praises to God for all his promises abideth forever. Although the enemy tried, God defended his own and in the end, you were not asked to return even one kobo of that eighty billion to the commonwealth of the Nigerian people.

Although I am not saying this to mock him, I cannot but cite the sorrowful case of Chief Lucky Igbinedion who had to refund a crushing amount of almost five million naira out of the thirty million dollars he transferred to his accounts overseas for safe keeping for the people of Edo state. There is also Chief Tafa Balogun who had to return almost two million naira and about five of his more than twenty houses and mansions. God did not make your own case to be like the cases of these two people. Chief Sir, you did not come to this world with two heads. You have only one head, just like Lucky Igbinedion and Tafa Balogun. We are not mocking them by comparing your situation with theirs. We are just praising God for his mercies on you. *A o fi yo won. Afi n gbe oruko Olorun ga ni.*

With eighty billion reasons in my mind sir, and given my firm belief that you are one of the leaders anointed by God to continue to lead this country after your minor tribulation, I am humbly applying, through this medium, to work for you when you get out of jail. Chief, I am applying to become your Senior Special Assistant on Bounce-Back and Re-Integration. Although you are yet to advertise any such position, it is easy to see that you will need somebody to function in that capacity when you get out.

My aptitude for this position is based on my thorough knowledge of the psychology of Nigerians. If you hire me, Chief, our greatest asset will be their memory. It is legendarily short and that is fantastic for the job at hand. All we need do is make it even shorter in order for you to bounce back with the bang that you truly deserve. To this end, I have worked out a number of measures hereunder summarised for you. If hired, I will obviously flesh them out in greater detail and pursue each goal vigorously to fruition.

The first thing we will need to arrange upon your release is a grand interdenominational thanksgiving service that will be attended by the proverbial Nigerian "dignitaries from all walks of life." You will have to ride to church on a white horse, surrounded by drummers, singers and a mammoth crowd of *aso-ebi* supporters. We will need to hold the church service in a football stadium – I suggest Ibadan. We could then rent and bus in supporters from all the states in the southwest and beyond to fill the stadium. I am currently preparing a draft of the testimony you will give during the service. You will basically say that you bear no grudge against anyone and you have forgiven Nigerians. You have accepted your ordeal as one of those personal sacrifices a true leader must make to move Nigeria forward. You will enjoin your enemies and persecutors to join hands with you to make Nigeria great. After the interdenominational service in Ibadan, you will pay a brief courtesy call to Daddy General Overseer on the Lagos-Ibadan expressway for photo-ops and additional spiritual fortification against dominions, powers and principalities. We will then proceed to Lagos for an all-night *owambe* party with King Sunny Ade performing. Fashola or no Fashola, we can still close a few roads in Lagos for the party. Not even Fashola will stand in the way of eighty billion naira in Nigeria. *Ngbati o ya were*! We will need about a billion naira for this phase.

With the Christian phase of the bounce-back strategies complete, we will proceed to the traditional phase. I propose here that we try to expand your already expansive portfolio of chieftaincy titles. It will be necessary for you to spend a few months crisscrossing Nigeria to gather chieftaincy titles all over the country. When you have done this, you will return to Yoruba land where we shall have to pay a courtesy visit to every important traditional ruler, reminding them that it is now time to fill Chief M.K.O Abiola's shoes by electing a new Aare Ona Kakanfo of Yoruba land. Personally, I do not know who fits the bill better than a retired military man with eighty billion naira – excluding assets and what you made as Governor of Ondo State. Chief, we could pull off this Aare Ona Kakanfo *thing* if we play our cards right. I suggest committing ten billion naira to this project.

Chief, you will also have to start a newspaper, for obvious reasons. Fortunately, we could tap into the newspaper-ownership experience of Governor Gbenga Daniel, Chief James Ibori, and even your adversary, Asiwaju Bola Tinubu. Pending the take-off of your newspaper, we will need to buy some plots of land in Abuja and distribute them to the editors of strategically important newspapers. It is also compulsory to invite Dele Momodu to lunch, not because we need him to splash your photos in Ovation but because he will devote a three-part panegyric essay to you that will run for three weeks in his column in *ThisDay* newspaper.

Allied to newspaper ownership, we would need to hire a gaggle of internet rats and plant them in strategic Nigerian chat rooms, discussion boards, listservs, and allied cyber spaces where Nigerians have been sending their restless mouths on all kinds of dirty errands against you. Ah, those people have spoilt your name online, sir! Depending on your relationship with Chief Ibori, we could get him to loan us the two extremely experienced internet rats on his payroll, Tony Eluemunor and Areh Sunday. These two fellas could potentially train whoever we hire. Besides, it shouldn't cost too much to get them on loan since they are already getting their share of the national cake from James Ibori. Your money and Ibori's money are from the same source – the Nigerian people. No one should be paid twice from the same source if they don't want to be guilty of double collection.

Chief, you will also need to become a serious godfather to facilitate your bounce back on the one hand and ensure that the eighty billion is constantly replenished on the other hand. Eighty billion naira may sound like a lot of money but Nigeria is a very expensive place. A man of your calibre—and whose reputation is now in tatters—needs to control the treasury of at least one state to remain buoyant. Fortunately, the onshore model of Olusola Saraki (Kwara), Lamidi Adedibu (Oyo), and Bola Tinubu (Lagos) is now out-dated. You no longer have to remain in your state to be a godfather and governor-installer in Nigeria. Chief Tony Anenih and Professor Charles Soludo have recently invented the concept of offshore godfathering that enabled Chief Anenih to leave Edo and ply his trade in Anambra.

As I do not see any southwest state where you could immediately overthrow the existing onshore godfather in the circumstances, my idea is to test the waters everywhere from the middlebelt to the far north, from the south-south to the southeast, to determine where you could become an offshore godfather. If we don't find a state where you could become the sole offshore godfather, we could try partnering. Chief

Chris Uba is so desperate to keep Soludo and Anenih out of his fief that he won't mind teaming up with you as offshore godfather. Since all you need is a share of the treasury and will not quarrel with him over appointments—you cannot come from Yoruba land and appoint commissioners in Anambra—he may be favourably disposed to the idea. We can agree to him having 50% of the state's monthly Federal allocation, you get 20%, and Anambra people will get the remaining 30% to sort out themselves. In fact, I suspect that Anambra will work for us since every politician with a dick in Nigeria now think they can piss generously on that state.

On a more personal level Chief…I don't even know how to say this… it is delicate. Well, you see, you have a young beautiful bride who got libidinous tongues wagging all over the internet when they saw her photo at your trial. That is a lesson in life, Chief. You are still alive and around and Nigerian men were already openly fantasising about your wife. Anyway, Chief, the young Roline will have to accept an even younger rival. Nothing says bounce back in Nigeria like becoming President Yar'Adua's son in-law. You may want to consider marrying one more time. The bad news: here is only one Presidential daughter left to dole out and we hear she already has a fiancée. I guess the only thing stopping the marriage is that they are yet to find a state for him, governorship of a state being a non-negotiable conditionality for marrying the President'0s daughters. This is why we are still lucky. We may be able to persuade the President and Madam Turai to modify that conditionality and expand it to include former governors.

This is a summarised and considerably condensed version of my road map for your bounce back. The full version is in my laptop, sir. If you hire me, I am willing to fly to Nigeria to discuss this with you in Kirikiri. That would be a good time to discuss my salary, inconvenience allowance since I will be relocating home from abroad, and other emoluments.

Yours sincerely,
Dr Makojami Olugbala.

Letter of Gratitude to Her Excellency Turai Yar'Adua

(April 2010)

Dear substantive Mama of our dear nation,

Greetings, ma. I call you substantive Mama of the nation to remind Patience Jonathan that you are still in charge, ma. She has been awfully quiet and unseen as you go through these trying times. That is bad news, ma. I would have preferred her to be visible and hyperactive now on the national social scene so that you could at least gauge what she is up to and keep an eye on her.

But I digress, ma. I am writing to thank you for little mercies and all the things you have done for Nigeria. Nigerians have been so unkind to you, ma. There is no name they have not given you. One Hausa-Fulani woman who writes *yeye* articles for Sam Nda Isaiah's *Leadership* like she is on the payroll of Wole Soyinka and Yinka Odumakin called you "megalomaniac Goldilocks." Some have called you Lady Macbeth or Imelda Marcos. If I got a kobo for every name you have been called since you took Alhaji to Saudi Arabia and successfully brought him back home, I wouldn't need to write this letter, ma.

That is my way of saying that I am not like those ungrateful Nigerians, ma. I always love to see a half full cup as opposed to those perennially negative Nigerians for whom the cup is always half empty. As they say, there is a silver lining in every situation. My eyes are specially designed to spot such linings. They don't even have to be silver for me to see them. That is why I am writing this letter to thank you on behalf of myself, my family and all those misguided Nigerians who are out there abusing you, ignorant of so many things you have done for our country even in your tribulation.

I'm a writer, ma. So let me start with what you have done for my constituency. Unknown to many people, the Yar'Adua era will be remembered as the finest hour of Nigerian literature. Those of us who are toilers in the vineyard of the imagination have never had it so good. Nigeria has been very hostile to literature and the imagination since Independence. Every major prize ever won by Nigerian writers—Nobel, Booker, Commonwealth, Orange, Noma—has been in spite and not because of the Nigerian state. Official Nigeria does not like stories. Official Nigeria hounds and imprisons writers. Official Nigeria has been known to hang a writer if he stands in the way of more important things, like oil.

But you have changed all that, ma. You have created an enabling environment in which the entire country is now ruled by stories. People make a mistake when they think that Acting President Goodluck Jonathan is now in charge. The only "entity" with full Presidential powers in Nigeria at the moment is what we call the Story in my line of work. The story rules. The story rocks. And through the story, writers and those who thrive on the imagination are now the effective rulers of Nigeria. Mind you, the story doesn't just rule, it has hegemony. Madam, something acquires hegemony when a large number of people recognise its authority and collectively subscribe to it. Hegemony happens, madam, when their behaviour is modified by their subscription to the authority of that thing.

What does this *dogon turenchi* mean, ma? It means that we have effectively been ruled, week in week out, by the stories you have so carefully authored and released since you got back from Saudi. Those stories acquire hegemony when we plug into them and subscribe to their authority. Left to me, you would be made Life Matron of the Association of Nigerian Authors for services rendered to the imagination. First was the story that you were going to have a meeting with Goodluck Jonathan shortly after you got back from Saudi. The whole nation plugged into that story, held its breath, and it acquired hegemony and ruled us for a week. Then there was the story about your mother-in-law anxious to see her son. That story too ruled us for a week. Then there was the story of one Katsina man who came to Aso Rock and allegedly strolled around with your husband. That one too ruled us for one week.

Then came the story of the empty presidential motorcade that was doing manoeuvres inside Aso Rock and even had Senators and Reps scampering to safety with their tails tucked between their legs. That one too ruled us for a week. Then there was the story of the Imams who visited your husband and prayed for him. That ruled us last week. This week, we are being ruled by the story of the visit of the Christian clergy to your husband. Next week, another story will begin its Presidential reign. But for his retirement, Pa T. M. Aluko would by now have completed the draft of a novel entitled *One Week One Story*. This is just to show how much you have done for the literary community. We are grateful for the endless and restless run of stories, ma.

Speaking of visits by Imams and Christian Pastors, I want to thank you for having faith in Nigerian Islam and Christianity. That is why you brought local Imams and Pastors to conduct the Presidential sighting in Aso Rock. Had you elected to do things the expected way, ma, you would have imported Imams and Ayatollahs from Saudi, Kuwait, Iran and Indonesia and later have them give their verdict on your husband to Nigerians on Al-Jazeera; you would have flown in T. D. Jakes, Benny Hinn and Reinhard Bonnke to perform the Christian sighting of your husband and have them announce their verdict on CNN. Imagine what it would have cost Nigeria if you had elected to fly in all these people. For using local Imams and Pastors and saving us so much money, I thank you from the bottom of my heart.

One other positive fallout of the Christian sighting expedition to Aso Rock that we need to thank you for is the manufacturing of a brand new Pentecostal superstar named Emmanuel Kure. Before this visit, Pastor Emmanuel Kure and his Throneroom Trust Ministry Inc were unknown quantities in Kaduna. Now, Enoch Adeboye, William Kumuyi, David Oyedepo, Chris Oyakhilome and Kris Okotie must welcome and make room for this latest entrant into Nigeria's celebrity Pentecostal pastorhood. By manufacturing and facilitating Pastor Emmanuel Kure's overnight superstardom ma, you have rendered an invaluable service to our country by correcting the unfairness inherent in southern domination of the Pentecostal market.

Until now, every celebrity ministry has been based on the Lagos-Ibadan expressway. Not even the periodic slaughter of witch-children by Helen Upkabio in Calabar has been able to break the monopoly that the Lagos-Ibadan expressway Daddy General Overseers have held over fame and the proceeds thereof for such a long time. Now you have created a new market in Kaduna. Apart from creating a geographical balance, it will also lead to a more equitable distribution of wealth. Ministers, Senators, Reps and Governors always take ten percent of their monthly loot to the Lagos-Ibadan expressway. Now, I foresee a situation where only five percent would go to Lagos-Ibadan expressway and five percent would go to Kaduna.

Ma, it is gratifying to note that your creation, Pastor Emmanuel Kure, has already contributed his own quota to national development by announcing a missing "amen" in the local media. Apparently, as Pastor Kure led Bishop Oyedepo and Archbishop Onaiyekan in prayer by your husband's bedside, there was a chorus of "amens." As everybody's eyes were closed, no one could say with certainty if one of the "amens" came from your husband. By publicly declaring your husband's alleged "amen" missing, Pastor Kure has saved us the embarrassment that overzealous presidential aides could potentially have caused us.

One cannot put it beyond such aides to go behind your back, record your husband's "amen", and send it to the BBC for broadcast to Nigerians in a crazy bid to please you. Imagine the national embarrassment of having oga address us again via the BBC. If your aides try that trick behind your back ma, it will backfire because the whole country knows now that your husband's amen is still officially missing and has not been sighted since it escaped the room unseen by the closed eyes of Pastor Kure and Bishops Oyedepo and Onaiyekan. Ma, you may want to announce a substantial cash reward for any Nigerian who finds your husband's "amen" and takes it to the nearest police station. The only problem: we would never really be able to confirm if it's your husband's "amen" since all those who could physically recognise it had their eyes closed when it escaped.

Finally ma, some typical Nigerian badmouthers have gone to town saying that it would be so much easier if you invite local TV cameras from NTA, Channels, AIT, and select journalists from our newspapers to come and "sight" your husband. These people would be grateful to you if only they knew the patriotic reasons behind your determination to keep Nigerian journalists away from your husband. If the revelations coming from Azugate at the *Punch* are anything to go by, Nigerian journalists—especially those at the upper echelons of the profession—do not come cheap *at all at all*.

Do these Nigerians now running their mouths imagine what the damage would be to our treasury if you had to assemble a cast of top editors from all our credible newspapers and news magazines and camera crews from our major TV stations? Do they think that those newspapers are going to send hungry rookie reporters who would be content with the conventional brown envelopes containing only a few thousands? We are in the big league here. We are talking about people who would require the sort of gargantuan settlement Aso Rock regularly gives to members of the National Assembly if they are to blast front page stories claiming that they played squash with the President. You are saving Nigerians a lot of money by keeping these people away and I'm grateful to you ma.

Em... em... one last thing, ma. You would have seen from this my very long letter that I am far better than Segun Adeniyi at this job of presenting your own side of the story to the Nigerian people. If he can no longer work for your husband's office, should he be told that he has to start working for you unofficially and unsolicited as proof of his loyalty? Instead of writing positive stuff like this about you, he went to watch the Nations Cup in Angola. Can you imagine, ma? At a time you needed him most, he was watching football in Angola. I'm not saying that you should sack him *o*, ma. I'm just saying that em… em… I'm better at these things. I even applied to Chief Olabode George for a job as his publicist but I never heard back from him. I suspect that the wardens at Kirikiri did not deliver my letter. That means that I'm still a jobless Ph.D holder ma. And available…

Yours sincerely,
Dr Makojami Olugbala.

Letter of Gratitude to Senator Iyiola Omisore

(December 2010)

To the accompaniment of Fela's "Look and Laugh"

Dear Distinguished Senator Chief Otunba Iyiola Omisore (OFR, MON, NTA, JCCR),

Calvary greetings to you, sir, in the name of our Lord Jesus Christ. I hope this letter meets you in good condition of health, if so, doxology. I am directed to write you this letter of gratitude on behalf of the long-suffering people of Nigeria. We want to thank you and your colleagues in the Senate for the enormous sacrifice you have made to ensure the democratisation of laughter in Nigeria. By returning mirth to the streets of Nigeria, you have broken rank with members of Nigeria's political leadership whose latest assault on the hapless people of Nigeria has been the exercise of a greedy capitalist monopoly on laughter.

Although some foreign researchers improved Nigeria's international image by famously describing us as the happiest people on earth, as opposed to our stubbornly unrebrandable image as the *yahoo-yahoo* capital of the world, it would seem that members of Nigeria's rulership were not happy with the extension of the new stereotype of happiness to every Nigerian. They don't like to share even sunlight and oxygen with the ordinary Nigerian. This attitude stems from their wholesale subscription to the philosophy of David Bonaventure Alechenu Mark:

Laughter is not for the poor. In their esteemed opinion, laughter ought to be the exclusive property of the rich, mighty and powerful in Nigeria.

The appropriation of laughter as elite property explains why only the insanely wealthy and politically powerful have been finding things funny in Nigeria of recent. The roll call is impressive. Former president Olusegun Obasanjo recovered in time from the blows he received at the Lagos Airport recently to make a transition from *dey-ing kampe* to *laughing o*. Not to be left out of elite "laffomania", Atiku Abubakar found time to laugh too *o*. The elite merrymakers had female company as Dora Akunyili laughed her way from Naija to Nigeria but not before abusing those of us that she left behind in Naija. Trust Dimeji Bankole to carry his yeye *Britico* 'fone' into the theatre of elite laughter and mirth for he too jokingly remarked that lawmakers are educated.

Enter Aso Rock with Godsday Orubebe (Is Elder part of his name or a reflection of the Naija big man's disdain for Mr?) laughing and scoffing at the idea that Nigerians could believe that somebody at his level would attempt to bribe anyone with something as ridiculous as fifty thousand dollars on behalf of a whole President and Commander-in-Chief of the Armed Forces of the Federal Republic of Nigeria. When we honour Bakin Zuwo's memory by ensuring that there is always some government money in government house to be used as gift and transport fare for friends and foes who visit the president, do these Nigerians imagine that we are talking about ordinary fifty thousand dollars? That's peanuts. We are talking of billions of petrodollars now firmly in the hands of the real owners of the petrol for God's sake. Why should they squander it only in thousands? Orubebe hasn't stopped laughing at just how cheap Nigerians could be.

Distinguished Senator Omisore sir, this is the scenario that you and your fellow Distinguished colleagues in Nigeria's Senate assessed and decided that it wasn't fair for the people of Nigeria to be left out of this orgy of elite laughter and mirth. The monopolisation of laughter by your fellow inhabitants of the planet of power and wealth grated your populist conscience. You were disturbed and you agonised about finding ways and means to reduce the suffering and hardship of the

Nigerian people by making them laugh. You decided that laughter would become the exclusive property of Obasanjo, Atiku, Akunyili, Bankole and Orubebe only over your dead body. You would fight for Nigerians and ensure that we gain access to our fair share of laughter and mirth. Sanusi Lamido Sanusi gave you the opportunity to come to our rescue.

Distinguished Senator Omisore sir, we have taken a sabbatical from our poverty and suffering, we have taken a break from fighting our never-ending Pentecostal wars against dominions, powers, and principalities just to have a really good laugh since your altercation with that obstreperous Central Bank Governor began. Even the stone and trees in Nigeria have not been left out of this national comic relief. They too have been laughing sir.

The national festival of laughter began, sir, when Nigerians discovered, much to their pleasant surprise, that you and your colleagues in the Senate seriously believed that Sanusi had tarnished the good image of the National Assembly. The Nigerian people somehow missed the memo and therefore did not know that the National Assembly had any image that could be tarnished in the first place by anybody. That's like Ibrahim Babangida complaining that his good name has been tarnished. That is why we laughed so hard, sir.

It got better. We also learnt that you and your colleagues feared that Mr. Sanusi might have incited the Nigerian people against the National Assembly. How do you incite the Nigerian people against what they consider the worst arm of a gangrened and irredeemably corrupt democracy? How do you incite the Nigerian people against the world's most corrupt, most indolent, most immorally overpaid parliament? How do you incite a people against lawmakers who inspire only contempt and disgust? We thought that we were already permanently incited against the National Assembly and didn't even realize that we needed Mr. Sanusi's help. You can see why we have been laughing so hard, sir.

I don't know how to say this, sir. I will be as delicate as I can be. Bear in mind that I am only reporting the mood of the Nigerian people to you. It's just that Nigerians laughed hard, so hard when it was eventually revealed that of all the people that the Senate could find to grill a mind like Sanusi Lamido Sanusi, it had to be you, Senator Iyiola Omisore! Sanusi combines the best in Arabic scholarship with Western political discourse and philosophy. If you study his essayistic career before he became a public figure, you will see that he quotes everybody from Antonio Gramsci to Michel Foucault via Plato, Ovid, Richard Rorty, and Paul de Man. I won't put it beyond the man to be reading Greek and Latin texts in the original. A man of such impeccable intellectual depth was going to be grilled by a National Assembly populated almost exclusively by school certificate forgers, Oluwole customers, University dropouts, active and retired political assassins, and puny election riggers. And this inquisition by intellectual midgets was going to be led by you, sir. We laughed so hard!

All good things, they say, must come to an end. Our week of laughter has now ended after your encounter with Sanusi went the way we knew it would go. We hear that your junior colleagues in the lower chamber have taken style to pipe down after seeing what Sanusi did to their seniors. Good for them. Dimeji Bankole sometimes accidentally demonstrates wisdom. He knows that when the horse leading the pack falls into a ditch, those following it must pause and proceed *jejely*.

On another note, it would help a lot, sir, if you paid an occasional visit to Nigeria to know what is going on there. You and your colleagues in the Senate fell into the fallacy of believing that the National Assembly had any image that could be tarnished because you seldom leave your planet of wealth and power in Abuja to check out what is going on in Nigeria. On the rare occasions that you visit Nigeria, the convoys, aides, girlfriends, and rifle-wielding soldiers keep Nigeria out of your range of vision. You can therefore be forgiven for not knowing what Nigerians think of the National Assembly.

Once again, thank you for bringing laughter to the streets of Naija this past week. Your work is greatly appreciated, sir.

Yours sincerely,
Professor Elder Otunba Makojami Olugbala (JP).

Part Four:

All the World's a Stage

Ebele, Take Time O!

(March 2010)

"Ebele, Ebele, Ebele wake up now. Honey, are you sleeping?"

"Sweetheart what is it now. . ." (Yawn) "What is it? You know how tough this Acting President job is. Baby, let me sleep now. Tomorrow, I have all kinds of meetings and..."

"And what, Ebele? And what?"

"Sweetheart, stop raising your voice now. Do you know what time it is?"

"Ebele, I'm sorry for you. If David Mark and Dimeji Bankole *dem* are deceiving you, I am your wife. I cannot follow to deceive you. You say we are President yet we are still in this house. They are in the main house."

"They? Who're they?"

"The Dalai Lama and Winnie Mandela! Look, Ebele *no vex me this night o*. What do you mean who's they?"

"Oh you mean..."

"The ghost and his wife, of course."

"Patience, must you always call him a ghost? And I keep telling you that I don't know how to evict them."

"You see now! And you call yourself a man? And you call yourself Acting President! Yet a common ghost and his madam are keeping us awake every night and you don't know how to evict them. Aso Rock *na* hospital or *na* hospice? Anyway, Ebele, *dat's* your own, me I want to sleep on that presidential bed *o*. Even if for one night. *Dis* one *dat* I have been telling you to try and see how we can be here after 2011, and you are doing *sme-sme.*"

"Patience, how many times will I tell you that these things are not as easy as you think? Even the PDP..."

"Which PDP? Are you not the party leader? Is it not Ogbulafor? It is because you won't give me free hand. Give me free hand to work with Bukola Saraki and James Ibori; give me free hand to resurrect and dust up Tony Anenih, Ahmadu Ali and Bode George; give me a budget. All of these men can be bought to our side once they sniff the possibility of power and influence for another eight years under you. You'll see that God works in miraculous ways."

"You women! You think that these things are just done like that."

"Okay *o*, Ebele, I have said my own. If you like, hear, if you like, don't hear. At least my conscience is clear that I am being a good wife by showing you the road. Since you won't take care of your portion, Ebele, what about my own portion?"

"Your own portion?"

"Ebele, what is wrong with you tonight? Why are you pretending not to understand anything I say? *Na jeje I siddon* as Second Lady of the Federation with all the perks of office and recognition of that title at public functions."

"But nothing has happened to your title, Patience."

"Don't make me lose my patience this night *o*, Ebele. What do you mean nothing has happened to my title? Since the National Assembly used *wuruwuru* to make you Acting President, I have been the only victim of the entire thing."

"Patience, for God's sake! How have you been a victim or the only victim?"

"Well, Nigerians still have their Nigeria, *abi*? So they are not victims. Because the arrangement is not perfect. Soyinka, Tunde Bakare and Yinka Odumakin still have reason to be doing what they like doing: making noise, so they are not victims. The governors got their excess money from the Federation Account, so they are not victims. Most of the ministers are coming back, so they are not victims. Turai is still on the presidential bed in the presidential bedroom, so she is not a victim. That leaves me; Ebele, just me."

"Patience, how are you a victim?"

"Ebele, this your new status has transformed me from Her Excellency the Second Lady of the Federal Republic to Her Excellency Designation Unclear of the Federal Republic!"

"How so?"

"Ebele, stop playing dumb with me *o*. What or who am I now? Acting First Lady since you are Acting President? First lady-in-waiting? Second lady in temporary suspension? Ebele, what am I?"

"You are my wife, the wife of the Acting President of the Federation. That is not enough for you?"

"Thank you, Ebele, but it is not enough for me. I will not follow you do *sme-sme*. Even Mrs. Shonekan was Her Excellency Interim First Lady of the Federation. Everybody has had a specific designation in that office. Why my own must be different, Ebele tell me *o*. If you prefer to share your portion with a ghost that no one has seen, I will not share my portion with the wife of the ghost. I want to possess my possession, Ebele. I want you to ask the National Assembly to declare me Acting First Lady of the Federation."

"Patience! Patience! Please stop it, Patience!!!!"

"Ebele, I've lost my patience. Why are you screaming my name? What have I said that is so bad? Ebele take time *o*, take your time this night."

The Tower of Nido

(June 2010)

(Aso Rock, some years ago.)

"Ahmadu, Tony and Bode, have you given any thought yet to 2003 and 2007? Once we neutralise that greedy and ambitious Atiku, what next? You guys must deliver my third term in 2007 *o*. And we need to start strategising early."

"Your Excellency Baba, I don't know about Ahmadu and Bode but you can trust me. They don't call me your Mr. Fix-it for nothing. I'm already thinking very far ahead."

"Baba, don't mind Tony *o*. I am the original Lagos boy here. Any other Bode George is a counterfeit. I know how to get these things done."

"Ah, Baba, I am still your one and only Alli must go. Don't worry. We are busy working on the project. Once we get Atiku out of the way, we can rattle the Maradona of Minna a little bit. We can arrest and shake up one of his sons a little to the right and a little to the left. With Atiku and Maradona out of the way, all the other jokers will get the message that there is no vacancy in Aso Rock until you have served three terms. *Who born dem*?"

"Okay, gentlemen. I trust the three of you. But there is still one problem. Even when we have taken care of things and covered our bases at home, what about those noisemakers abroad?"

"You mean meddlesome foreign governments? Baba, I can fix them too. I don't just fix domestic irritations for you."

"Tony, who is talking about foreign governments? I mean Nigerians abroad. Ever since they found a mission and a coherent voice during their opposition to Abacha, they have become a force Abuja can no longer ignore. And you know that the *ipata* literature man from my neck of the woods in Ogun state is not helping matters."

"Baba, you mean the restless Professor who wears a white mane on his head?"

"Yes *o*. My so-called friend and kinsman! At his age, he is still roaming Western capitals, mobilising Nigerian communities in Euro-America against us. And you know they listen to him. Once he suspects that we are already thinking of a third term, you can trust him to hop on the plane and begin to mobilise Nigerians all over Europe and America."

"I see your point, Baba. The internet too is not helping matters. It has given those noise making Andrews abroad a capacity for mobilisation and a presence they didn't have just a few years ago. Our foreign partners are now into the irritating habit of even feeling the pulse of their guest Nigerian communities before doing business with us."

"Ha ha ha ha ha ! He he he he he! Hu hu hu hu hu!"

"Am I missing something here? What's funny? What's wrong with the three of you?"

"Baba, it's the importance you accord to Nigerians abroad that we find so funny. What you are mistaking for their unity of purpose is actually just a case of the loquacious ones among them having a reason to scream about the same thing at the same time: Abacha, corruption, no water, no light, no infrastructure, *bla bla bla*. It is just a unity of convenience. I can fix it into disunity if that becomes necessary for our objective."

"I agree with Tony. Baba, you and I are both Yoruba. May I respectfully remind you of the Yoruba practice of finding '*ai roju, ai raye*' for any irritant or upstart who gets in your way? We also call it the philosophy of '*j'en raye se temi*'. All we have to do is find original '*ai roju, ai raye*' for those noisemakers who call themselves Nigerians abroad and we shall '*raye se tiwa*' here in Abuja."

"Tony, you see these Yoruba people now? There are four of us here. Only Baba and Bode are Yoruba and they are both blowing Yoruba philosophy! Anyway, Bode, I presume we are part of this plan? So translate all your Yorubawa abeg."

"Okay, Tony and Ahmadu, when *ai roju, ai raye* is deployed as a strategy to achieve *j'en raye se temi*, it means you find work for your enemy. You keep him so busy, distracted and disorganised that it becomes impossible for him to focus on you. When your enemy does not *roju* and does not *raye*, you are free to pursue your own agenda."

"Fantastic! Excellent! With all due respect to you, Baba, you see why I fear Yoruba people now?"

"We, Yoruba, *dey kampe*, Tony. Fear us. Anyway, Bode, I am going to Atlanta next month. And I hear that I will have a huge Town Hall meeting with Nigerians from all over the United States. That could be an opportunity to launch operation *ai roju raye*. What exactly do you have in mind?"

"Excellent! I'm beginning to like this! Baba, if you ask me, the only way to ensure their disunity is actually to unite them."

"Bode, speak English to us. What is all this paradox? Is it because we mentioned the *ipata* literature man with the famous white mane?"

"Sorry, Baba. What better way to disunite Nigerians than to bring them together from across our volatile ethnic fault lines and ask them to run something together? Let's give them a well-funded organisation to run. We'll humour some gargantuan egos in the Nigerian community out there with the usual speeches about taking them seriously and wanting them to partner with the Federal government to move Nigeria forward."

"*Chei*, Bode, you are a genius. As national chairman of our great party, I say this with a great sense of responsibility. Baba, Bode's plan could help us kill two birds with one stone."

"How so, Ahmadu?"

"Baba, we all know that a group of Nigerians from across the ethnic fault lines cannot possibly run an organisation without bringing down the roof with the usual Nigerian factor. Now, those loud Nigerians in Europe and America have this irritating habit of looking down pompously on those of us at home. They abuse us all the time and accuse us of incompetence. We can't run Nigeria *bla bla bla* and more *bla*. Let's give them an organisation of their own to run. We all know that they will make a mess of it right there abroad. And we would have demystified them, apart from distracting them from our agenda. If they can't run a small organisation abroad, they won't have any moral basis to run their mouths about the incompetence of those of us running Nigeria at home."

"So, are we going to form this organisation for them? That could backfire."

"Of course not, Baba! We shall induce its formation and fund it heavily. But we shall make them think that they formed it of their own volition. When their leaders come to Abuja, we give them an official car, a driver, some assistants, and accommodation in a Federal government guest house. Just give them some sense of importance and the illusion that they are relevant to anything here at home. But beyond all that, the Federal government shall maintain perfect deniability at all times."

"Okay, I'm beginning to like this plan. Who do we need to get operation *ai roju raye* off the ground?"

"Apart from the four of us here, we have to proceed on a need-to-know basis. We need to brief our men on the ground in the US, Jibril Aminu and Joe Keshi, immediately. They can begin the spade work for the formation of some kind of umbrella organisation of Nigerians abroad as part of the highlights of your trip to Atlanta, sir."

"Will they be in on the real plan?"

"*Haba*, Baba! Of course not! They don't need to know. Let's just tell them that we need them to facilitate the formation of a Nigerians in Diaspora Organisation, NIDO. They need not know anything beyond that. Once it gets off the ground, the Nigerian factor should hopefully set in. Egos will clash and, in no time, the principal actors will turn it to a Nigerians in Disarray Organisation. And that would just be perfect for us."

"This is just great! Bode, you are at the Ports. Fund operation *ai roju raye*. Presidential order. No spending cap. And, remember, the Federal government has no hand whatsoever in the formation of the organisation."

(Some years later, a NIDO meeting in progress somewhere in North America...)

"Ladies and gentlemen, let's have some quiet please. The hall is too rowdy. Let's not turn NIDO to the tower of Babel. May I remind you all that during the last NIDO elections held in Texas..."

"Shut up! You and who held elections in Texas?"

"Hey Mister, you shut up. That was rude of you to interrupt the MC like that. You did not have the floor."

"The floor my foot! How can he be talking about elections in Texas? No, we did not hold elections. We merely nearly did."

"Good talk, my broda. I support you. No election was held in Texas. Besides, the NIDO meeting we are talking about was held in Washington, not Texas."

"Ah yes, I remember now! That's when we formed the Lo Losun committee..."

"Lo Losun committee *ko*, Lo Laro committee *ni*. We did not form any Lo Losun committee in Washington!"

"Yes, we did! It was an ad hoc committee mandated to look into the NIDO imbroglio in New Jersey where one female Christian Taliban has been a bull in a china shop."

"My friend, that was not a committee *o*. That was a board."

"No, it was a committee."

"I say na board."

"I say no be board. Na committee."

"Ah, okay, yes we formed a committee. But it was not set up to look into the episodic pockets of NIDO crises in New Jersey and other

NIDO hot spots in the United States and Canada. I think you are talking about the Stakeholder A. Y. Hamis ad hoc committee which was mandated to look into the immediate, intermediate, and remote possibilities of amalgamating the multiple crises from NIDO Americas to NIDO South Africa via NIDO Europe and blend them all into one harmonious and manageable crisis. Check the minutes. I'm sure I'm right."

"No. You are wrong. The Stakeholder A. Y. Hamis ad hoc committee was formed to conduct a census of all the warring factions, sub-factions, semi-factions, mini-factions, and counter-factions of each NIDO chapter that we currently have in all the accredited regions. The committee for the amalgamation of NIDO crises worldwide that you are referring to was headed by someone else. Not the venerable Stakeholder A. Y. Hamis."

"Ah yes, you are right! I remember we drank so much coffee at that meeting."

"Coffee *ke*? We did not drink coffee *o*. We drank tea. Are you sure you were at that meeting?"

"My friend, I know what I'm saying. We drank coffee."

"No sir, we drank tea."

"Coffee!"

"Tea!"

"Are you trying to say that I'm lying, you *inyanmirin* son of a bitch? Who even brought these *okoro* boys to NIDO sef? I'm sure the Shylocks only came because of our Abuja land bonanza."

"Eh, eh, eh, see this semi-illiterate *ofem manu* Yoruba bastard and *ngbati* traitor who does not even know the difference between coffee and tea! And he is talking to me! No be your fault. Na NIDO. Abuja land bonanza my foot. *No be your greedy ngbati people chop all di land*?"

"Gentlemen, behave, please! We are not in the tower of Babel. And may I remind you that the controversy over our Abuja land bonanza has now been rested? Can we please get to our business of the day now? Remember we are here to discuss the dissolution of the current Exco..."

"*Fa fa fa foul*! You and who agreed to dissolve which Exco? Do you guys even read our Constitution at all? The current Exco has two more years in office!"

"I thought we covered this ground before. Why this attempt to sit-tight and extend the life of the current Exco beyond what our Constitution allows?"

General commotion in the house. Shouts of "We no go gree, nsobu nsobu eyimba eyimba, and bole dija ko dija, bole dogun ko dogun" can be heard all over the room. Some members storm out...

(A few days later...)

COMMUNIQUE

We, the Committee of Progressive NIDO Chieftains, Stakeholders, and Elder Statesmen, wish to announce the formation of a new chapter of the organisation to be known as NIDO Washington District of Columbia chapter – not to be confused with NIDO Washington DC chapter. NIDO District of Columbia has had to sadly split from NIDO DC owing to irreconcilable differences...

The Lonely Charlatans

(December 2010)

(To the accompaniment of Akon's "Lonely")

"Hello, hello, hello... ah, this call is not going through. Maybe the network is bad in Abeokuta... hello, hello, hello, ehen, it is ringing now."

"Hello, who is speaking please?"

"Hello... *line yen o clear dada...* hello, is that my brother, His Excellency Ogidi Omo?"

"Yes, this is His Excellency OGD. Who is this please?"

"Ah, don't you recognise my voice? This is me, My Excellency Oyato. I'm calling from Ibadan."

"Ah!!! Your Excellency my brother! *Oyato fun ra e! O ma t'ojo meta.* So nice to hear from you. Did you say you were calling from Ibadan? I thought you were taking a few days off to rest in Ogbomoso?"

"Ah, rest ke? *Ogbomoso ko, Alimosho ni.* How can you even talk about rest with all the *yanpon yanrin* that is happening to us?"

"Your Excellency, take it easy. What seems to be the problem?"

"Ogidi Omo my brother, are you an Oyo man? What is this amoran bini Oyo business? Why ask me questions when you and I are in the same boat and you know that we should be looking for ways to re-bury the corpse."

"Brother Oyato, re-bury the corpse? Which corpse?"

"Yes, brother OGD, the corpse that our great party buried in the dead of night in the southwest now has its two legs exposed in broad daylight. We must cover the exposed legs with fresh sand quick quick before further damage is done."

"Brother Oyato, you speak in riddles."

"Brother OGD, all I'm saying is that water has filtered into the snail's mouth from the rear and we must do something about it."

"Brother Oyato, I say you speak in proverbs. *E tu mi nle.*"

"Hmm, brother OGD, I am not the one speaking in proverbs *o*. It is political death that is addressing both of us in proverbs. Political death snarls at us in riddles."

"Political death? How so my brother?"

"Political death roamed the land and knocked on Professor Osunbor's door in Benin. The man said, 'Not I', but death spat on entreaties of money and kolanut. Political death knocked on Segun Agagu's door in Akure. The man said, 'Not I', but death spat on entreaties of money and kolanut. Political death knocked on Segun Oni's door in Ado Ekiti. The man said, 'Not I', but death spat on entreaties of money and kolanut. Political death knocked on Olagunsoye Oyinlola's door in Osogbo. The man said, 'Not I', but death spat on entreaties of money and kolanut. And when our elders in Abeokuta and Ogbomoso sat down and saw what we couldn't see standing, they exclaimed — Hun, hun, hun, when political death claims your neighbours and kinsmen, children, listen very carefully for you must know him when the husband of *arun* speaks to you in proverbs. OGD, *iku to p'ojuba eni, owe l'on pa fun ni.* I don't like what is happening all around us at all. It's getting quite lonely around here."

"Ah, my broda Oyato, I didn't realise you were talking about these tragic developments in the southwest. I've been thinking about it too. *Oro na o tie ye mi rara.*"

"Thinking? My brother OGD, did you say you have been thinking? Well, thinking is a luxury you can afford in Abeokuta because you have eaten for almost eight years now. Here in Ibadan, I am just about to eat for only four years and this Asiwaju man in Lagos is ruining everything for us."

"Ah, my broda, who told you that I am satisfied with just eight years? *Nkan eni ki di pupo ka binu.* My brother, I have worked very hard to put a formidable structure in place so that one of my boys could take over for the next eight years and guarantee the eating. So, I am as worried as you are by these negative developments in Yoruba land."

"Now you are talking. I wasn't even thinking of ordinary eight years in my case. Chief Vincent Ogbulafor assured us of sixty years. I sort of hoped that my grandchildren would be eating long after my body would have embraced its wrapper of sand. The most painful part is the behaviour of Baba in Ota. Instead of taking steps to address this ugly situation in Yoruba land, the man is busy laughing at Atiku. Our house is crumbling here in the West and the man is laughing *o*. Only God knows what the airport beating he got recently did to him. Baba is fumbling big time o. Iyen na ni Fayose fi ri won fin."

"My broda, Baba's case is even better. What about the fedora man in Abuja? What has he done for us? I mean, your party is losing an entire region to a tribunal revolution and you are grinning in Abuja and attempting to buy non-buyable troublemakers with $50,000. I never knew that I would see the day when our great party would be led by an incompetent briber."

"Don't mind him. As if he doesn't know how you have solved the problem of non-buyable troublemakers in Ogun in the last 8 years. Anyway, he is not an incompetent briber when he is directly affected *o*. He knows how to sell houses in Abuja to buy the leadership of the National Assembly or distribute any excess from the Federation account to buy our Governors' Forum."

"I am not even saying that armed robbers should attack and accidentally kill non-buyable troublemakers at the federal level. I am not sure he has what it takes to use the ***Dagger and Dart Direct*** method. But he could have done something about Ekiti and Osun all the same. He could have seconded Justice Ogebe temporarily to those tribunals on national assignment. That respected Supreme Court judge at least hears and speaks the language of our great party."

"So, my broda, how do we find a joint solution to this problem?

Here in Ibadan, I am rebuilding Tokyo's and Baba Adedibu's old structures to deal with that Asiwaju man. I am also considering banning those small boys, Mimiko, Fayemi and Aregbesola, from ever passing through Ibadan. *Awon alakori to fe gbaje l'enu wa.*"

"Broda Oyato, I think we should find some work for the Asiwaju before we deal with his boys. Maybe we should try to revamp that little University of Chicago certificate matter? Chief Gani Fawehinmi was looking into it but the man rented an *aso ebi* mob to sing *'yio sh'agolo d'Ondo'* and harass the respected Chief in the streets of Lagos. Maybe we could encourage Farida Waziri to pick up from where Chief Fawehinmi stopped? The case was never tidily concluded. Luckily for us, Farida Waziri is very encourageable in these matters."

"Wonderful! This is why I like you, broda OGD! *Elo ni*?"

"Elo ni what?"

"*Elo ni Waziri*?"

"Oh, *Waziri o won pupo ju*. She is very affordable. One customised Mercedes Benz jeep should do it. If she does a good job and gives Asiwaju the sort of *wahala ton pa lekun*, we could add *jara* to it for her. Maybe a plot of land here in Abeokuta or Ibadan. We could get Julius Berger to develop it for her."

"Good idea. You get the jeep. I will find her a plot of land here in Ibadan. What about that Yoruba boy who works for her, the noisemaker, Babafemi abi ki lo l'oun nje na?"

"That boy now..."

"Eehn o, That boy! *Se boy yen m'owo we*?"

"When you look at that boy's mouth, you know that he must know how to wash his hands properly."

"In that case, we can invite him to eat with elders. *A le ba oun na d'ogbon si*. I'm sure he's a good boy."

"With Waziri and Babafemi unleashed, *Asiwaju ru'gi oyin*!"

"I feel better already! Who says *egbinrin ote* does not pay? Now, OGD, what about these foolish boys all around us? Already, Fayemi, Mimiko and Aregbesola are holding meetings and talking about Awolowo's programmes. If they go and level up their states with Lagos and Edo, they will embarrass the two of us *o*. *Asiri wa a tu o*."

"Broda Oyato, you are right! I miss Uncle Tony Anenih, Uncle Bode George and Uncle Ahmadu Ali. *Mo j'eri won*! If only this clueless fedora man would recycle and bring them back into the game, they would know how to recapture the southwest."

"Maybe we should organise a little *operation wetie* here and there in Ondo, Ekiti, and Osun. If they are busy with riots and violence, they won't have time for development. Let's keep them busy with *ai r'oju ai r'aye. What do you think?"*

"Shhhhhhh, broda Oyato, stop talking like this on the phone! E fe ko ba wa ni? You will get us into trouble *o*. Those are strategies we should meet and discuss behind closed doors."

"But we are safe now. Nobody can hear us."

"Brother Oyato, ever heard of *Wikileaks*?"

*Where is that Bast**d?*

(February 2011)

"Where is the bastard? I say where is that bastard?"

"Baba, baba, baba, take it easy now. Bastard *wo l'en wa kiri* sir? We are in a church for thanksgiving *o*."

"Church my foot! If not for Olagunsoye Oyinlola who has been thanking God per second per second since he left office in Osogbo, I wouldn't be here in Okuku to risk being insulted by that boy a second time. The last time Oyinlola thanked God for a successful tenure of office, that bastard boy came here to abuse me."

"Baba, *e ni suru* sir."

"No, *mi o le ni suru rara* at all. I'm in no mood to *dey kampe* today. Now that we are here again to thank God for Oyinlola at sixty, that bastard may barge in at any time and disgrace me again. Imagine that boy calling me names the other time. I wonder who gave him pounded yam and told him that egusi soup was a cakewalk."

"But Baba. . ."

"Don't but me any *buts* my friend! Do I look like I *dey* laugh to you? If I don't deal with that boy once and for all today, he may be rude to me if Oyinlola invites us here again next week to thank God for his senatorial ambition."

"Baba, stop worrying about him, for God's sake. He is not here. He is running for the Senate and is busy campaigning in Ekiti."

"Is that not part of the nonsense that we are talking about in this country? We are planning to send all of our outgoing PDP governors to the retired governors' pension home that is the Senate and that bastard is trying to do the same thing in the Labour Party. Can you imagine a boy who called me a father of bastards planning to retire to the Senate in this country?"

"Baba, please stop worrying about that Ekiti rascal. Even if he wins, he will not get to Abuja. *Se b'awa ni.* Let's worry about the Emperor of Oke Mosan who is thumbing his nose at you in Ota."

"See me *o*. That is how this country treats elder statesmen. *Emi si Gbenga*! Because he has a richer wardrobe than his elders, he now imagines he also has more rags than his elders. I will teach that boy a lesson he will never forget. Good thing Oyinlola did not invite him here today."

"Shhhh, Baba, the Pastor is looking at us *o*. Let's listen to the sermon. . ."

My brothers and sisters, distinguished chieftains, stakeholders and elder statesmen of the PDP gathered to celebrate and felicitate with our brother, His Excellency General Chief Olagunsoye Oyinlola, on the occasion of his 60th birthday, you are most welcome to our church. I say unto you all: Nothing happens by accident. Everything is of God and has been pre-ordained by Him. God pre-ordained things and that is why you conquered this nation and captured power in 1999, 2003, and 2007. I tell you, nobody shall dispossess you of your possession in 2011, for I saw your dominion over this nation spread till eternity in a vision. For it is written in the book of Deuteronomy 7: When the LORD thy God shall bring thee into the land whither thou goest to possess it, and hath cast out many nations before thee, the Hittites, and the Girgashites, and the Amorites, and the Canaanites, and the Perizzites, and the Hivites, and the Jebusites, seven nations greater and mightier than thou;

And when the LORD thy God shall deliver them before thee; thou shalt smite them, and utterly destroy them; thou shalt make no covenant with them, nor shew mercy unto them:

Neither shalt thou make marriages with them; thy daughter thou shalt not give unto his son, nor his daughter shalt thou take unto thy son.

For they will turn away thy son from following me, that they may serve other gods: so will the anger of the LORD be kindled against you, and destroy thee suddenly.

But thus shall ye deal with them; ye shall destroy their altars, and break down their images, and cut down their groves, and burn their graven images with fire.

For thou art a holy people unto the LORD thy God: the LORD thy God hath chosen thee to be a special people unto himself, above all people that are upon the face of the earth.

Distinguished chieftains, stakeholders, and elder statesmen of the PDP, even as it happened unto the chosen ancients in the Bible, I command it today that so shall you smite and vanquish the ACN, the ACPN, the Labour Party, the CPC, and all the other enemies of your sixty-year inheritance in 2011...

"This is a good Pastor *o*. He is talking a lot of sense. Where did Oyinlola rent him? We need to do something for this church. How much seed should we sow during offering?"

"Ten million naira should be enough, Baba."

"Okay, I will do it but remind me to collect my money from the PDP national secretariat *o*. I am not sowing the seed in my private capacity *o*. Anyway, we were talking about Gbenga…"

"Yes *o*, Baba, since all these *small small* boys with a little change in their pockets are challenging us and rocking the boat left, right and centre, what are you our elders doing about it in the Board of Trustees? Since Jonathan is always doing *sme-sme*, I don't think you should entrust him with our do-or-die strategy as we approach April *o*."

"Who will trust that woman with do-or-die? He has messed up every do-or-die assignment thus far."

"Baba, which woman are you talking about?"

"Goodluck Jonathan of course. Didn't you just say he is always doing *sme-sme* like a woman? Ordinary to transfer and neutralise Justice Ayo Salami of the Court of Appeal, Jonathan and Katsina-Alu have bungled that vital anticipatory action in our do-or-die strategy. We have the Supreme Court firmly in our pockets because Katsina-Alu and Ogebe are our boys but that Ayo Salami won't let us have the Court of Appeal."

"Baba, knowing Jonathan and his *sme-sme*, the BOT should not have entrusted him with that delicate assignment."

"I didn't want to give that assignment to Jonathan but Andy Uba, Chris Uba, Ahmadu Ali, Tony Anenih and other party elders persuaded me to let the president look presidential by appearing to be in charge of things. We told him that Ayo Salami needs to go if we are to secure a landslide of judicial victories after April. He handed that delicate assignment over to Katsina-Alu and see what they have done."

"What would you have done, Baba?"

"I would have gotten my friend, Ban Ki Moon, to find him something at the International Court of Justice in the Hague. An important UN position that the stubborn judge would not have been able to resist because that would translate to Nigeria losing that slot at the international level. I have asked Jonathan to look into that possibility since the promotion to the Supreme Court option has blown up in our faces."

"Baba, move closer and let me whisper an idea into your ears… what about…*em*… *em*… I mean what about the Esa Oke protocol? We are still the PDP, aren't we? Our anticipated landslide victories will never be safe after April so long as that Ayo Salami is allowed to hang around *o*. My only fear is that if we use the Esa Oke protocol, that restless Professor who wears a white mane will go about calling us a nest of killers."

"Is that why you are whispering? This is a family gathering. Babangida is here. Alao Akala is here. Segun Oni is here. Segun Agagu is here. That Ekiti bastard is not here. Only our inner caucus people are here. There is nothing we cannot discuss openly in Oyinlola's *sakani*."

"Baba, the wall has ears."

"What is the world coming to? You are throwing proverbs around in front of an elder without permission. Is that how you were raised?"

"Apologies, Baba. Ah, the Pastor is looking our way again. I think we are talking too loud. Let's join the hymn."

Count your blessings name them one by one
Count your blessings see what God hath done
Count your many blessings
Name them one by one

And it will surprise you what the lord hath done

"Baba, as I was saying, we cannot talk with the full complement of our mouths here because the wall has ears. Baba, this place is infiltrated by the ears of the Asiwaju *o*."

"Ehn, Asiwaju *ke*?"

"Yes, there are suspicious elements in this church. Asiwaju will go to any length to infiltrate a gathering like this."

"This Oyinlola has gone soft *o*. How can he allow Asiwaju's ears to infiltrate this space? Are you sure that Kayode Fayemi, Raji Fashola, and even Rauf Aregbesola are not here?"

"*Haba* Baba!"

"That is why I was looking for that bastard Ekiti boy. If only he had come here today. I came prepared for him."

"Baba, this Pastor will drive us out of his church today *o*. He is frowning at us again. Let's listen a little."

...in conclusion of my ministration today, brothers and sisters, let us all rise up and say in unison to our dear brother, His Excellency General Chief Olagunsoye Oyinlola, even as he places his new political direction in the hands of the most high at sixty, let us all say to him along with the prophet Isaiah: 'Arise, shine, for your light has come, and the glory of the LORD is risen upon you. See, darkness covers the earth and thick darkness is over the peoples, but the LORD rises upon you and his glory appears over you. . .'

"Remind me to recommend this Pastor to Jonathan as the next chaplain of the Aso Rock chapel. He is a man of God in whom I am well pleased. He knows what to say."

"Okay, Baba, I will remind you. As I was saying, forget the Ekiti rascal. He is not here. Only his wife came to represent him."

"Ehn, *iwo omode yi*, what did you just say?"

"Oh, Baba, I said that his wife is here."

"At this thanksgiving service?"

"Yes, Baba."

"Why didn't you say so? And we have been here talking politics and Jonathan and Ayo Salami. I will never understand you boys of nowadays. Always leaving the best wine until past the midnight hour."

"*Em*, Baba, I don't understand why you are getting so excited *o*."

"Didn't you just say that the woman is here alone?"

"Yes, Baba, she is here to represent her husband. I think Oyinlola asked the Ekiti rascal to stay away out of respect for you so he sent his wife to represent him."

"And she came here alone? All by herself?"

"Yes, Baba."

"Lovely. Wonderful."

"Baba, I don't understand."

"No, my son, you don't understand."

"Baba, I hope it is not what I'm thinking. Why must you think that every woman's destiny is under your loins? Even Femi Fani-Kayode said that Saminu Turaki and co were supplying..."

"You see now? In the end, you are no different from that Ekiti boy who insulted me. You dare to open your rotten mouth and talk about my loins."

"Baba, I'm just saying that you should control it and not think that every woman, married or unmarried, is..."

"You are a bastard!"

Bode, Tibi Nko?

(March 2011)

(In the compound of a sprawling mansion in Lagos. Riotous singing and drumming by *aso ebi*-clad supporters.)

A ti nreti re, ka'abo se dada lo de
A ti nreti re, ka'abo se dada lo de
★★★
Winner o o o winner
Winner o o o winner
Lagos Boy you don win o winner
Patapata you go win forever
Winner
★★★
Odale se se se oju ti won o eh
O ma se oju t'elegan o
L'oju a mo koko bi kile o d'amo
O ma se oju t'elegan o

"Madam Roli, Madam Roli, can you tell our people outside to reduce the noise? I am trying to have a word with Bode on behalf of the Elders' Caucus of the PDP. We need to debrief your husband."

"Okay, Baba, I will tell them. I hope your people are fine in Ota, sir,"

"*O kare iyawo wa*. Well done, our dear wife. *Ku afoju ba* once again. Your husband is looking younger even after the enemies have done their worst."

"Em... Baba, Roli is my wife o. Not our wife. I'm still alive *abeg*. I only went to jail. Anyway, Roli, *se awon supporters won yen ti jeun*? They've eaten? Good. Tell them to reduce the noise like Baba said. Tell them we are expecting twelve more trailers of cows tomorrow for distribution to each ward. The remaining five trailers of *aso ebi* should be reserved for the women's delegation coming from Abuja."

"Bode, once again, *ka'abo*. You are welcome. We thank God. Where are the traitors behind your travails today? *Awon da loni*? One languished in a hospital in Saudi Arabia before returning home to meet his maker. The rest of that rude and power drunk cabal is history. They did all this to you just to get at me. *Awon afore su ni se buruku*."

"*Baba, e ku ile* once again. I am so happy to be back with you and I am moved to tears by all the support from our people. Our convoy could hardly move through the crowd of supporters. We even performed better than when Alamsco returned from London to the warm of embrace of his people in Bayelsa. God has really honoured us. But where are Gbenga and Ayo? They came to the church and should have followed us home in the convoy."

(Baba laughs.)

"Why? Am I missing something?"

"Ah, Bode, see what prison has done to you. God *soda* Yar'Adua's mouth wherever he is. I thought they allowed you to read newspapers and watch TV in the presidential wing of Kirikiri that we arranged for you?"

"I still don't understand what I am missing here."

"Well, all lizards lie prostrate. How to tell the one with a bellyache?"

"Meaning?"

"Haba, Bode, you no longer know the meaning of all lizards lie prostrate? *A ni gbogbo alangba lo danu de le*. Just because you saw Gbenga Daniel and Ayo Fayose in church does not mean that they are still with us."

"*O ti o*. Those are our boys now!"

"Ah, Bode, things happened while you were away! *Iya je mi*! You won't believe that Gbenga became so power drunk and arrogant that he started pointing in the direction of Ota with his left hand!"

"Haba, Baba, Gbenga cannot do that to you. He cannot do that to us! *Mo j'eri e*. Gbenga is a river that came into being before our very eyes. How can its currents sweep one away?"

"That's what my eyes saw *o*, Bode, but *I still dey kampe sha*."

"So Gbenga is truly misbehaving? What happened? We were around when that boy was born. *Oju wa na se bi*. We even watched him grow up. *Awa la wo d'agba*. How can he turn against you, Baba?"

"That is life for you, Bode. Osoba won that election but we did our usual do and gave Gbenga egusi soup but he has now drenched his chest with palm oil. But Gbenga's own is even small *o*. The *arifin* I have been receiving from Fayose is worse."

"Ehn, Ayo Fayose too?"

"Yes o, I don't even know the mouth with which to tell that one's story. That bastard saw me in Okuku and called me a father of bastards."

"*Eewo*! Abomination! Fayose said that to you?"

"Look, Bode, today is not the day to talk about all these useless boys that we picked up from the gutter and made governors. We have work to do. We have so much lost territory to reconquer. We lost most of the southwest in your absence. And Fashola has been behaving here in Lagos like the rat that became a landlord in the absence of the cat."

"This is all so depressing, Baba. How did we lose Ekiti, Ondo and Osun? Where was Goodluck Jonathan?"

"Jonathan? Bode, please don't mention tails in the presence of frogs. I have been trying hard to use patience in my dealings with that man."

"And it's not working? Didn't they say that she controls the man?"

"Who is talking about his wife? I mean one needs patience to deal with Goodluck because of his perpetual *sme-sme*. He has been misbehaving on the do-or-die front. He is not delivering at all. For instance, he was supposed to have announced a presidential pardon for you as part of a process of national healing before our convoy arrived here from church. That is what we instructed him to do. We also asked him to upgrade your national honour to GCON. Once your rehabilitation is complete, I am thinking of retiring and handling over the mantle of Founder of Modern Nigeria to you."

"That is true o. I am surprised that he hasn't announced my presidential pardon yet. Maybe he wants to announce it when I join him for breakfast in the Villa next week."

"He has surrounded himself with too many drunken fishermen sailors who are talking nonsense and making him wobble and fumble through every assignment we give him. Just imagine what he did with our winning formula for the April elections."

"What's the formula, Baba?"

"As you know, we are going to win the election the usual way and we expect Buhari, Ribadu, and Utomi to go to court as usual after addressing press conferences with my friend, Jimmy Carter. We know what will happen when they get to the Supreme Court because the judgement to be read by Katisna-Alu and supported by Ogebe will be written by some of my boys in Ota. In fact, we already have anticipatory drafts and Katsina-Alu will be in Ota to practise judgement delivery next week. Our only problem is the Court of Appeal where Justice Ayo Salami has refused to play ball so far. We asked Goodluck to take care of that problem."

"That's a small problem *now*."

"That's what we thought. Jonathan outsourced the assignment to Katsina-Alu and they somehow bungled it. The whole thing exploded in our faces, causing untold embarrassment. Now, the man is still there as President of the Appeal Court and that could cause a lot of problems for us in April."

"That's true, Baba. That is one problem we need to solve immediately. Why didn't they just use the Esa Oke protocol? Didn't anyone think of that?"

"Of course, we thought of the Esa Oke protocol. One of my boys even mentioned it to me again recently during Oyinlola's birthday thanksgiving in Okuku but after careful consideration, we decided to just take that option off the table for now."

"That's good, Baba, but I hope that Anenih, Andy Uba, Ahmadu Ali, Babangida and all our other people are aware that we may need to put that option to good use after April..."

"Yes, our people are fully aware of that. Let's talk serious business *jare*. Bode, *tibi nko*?

"*Tibi*?"

"Yes, Bode, what about *tibi*? Where is *tibi*?"

"Baba, I don't understand the *tibi* that you are talking about *o*."

"Bode, you just love to joke with serious matters. Abeg, talk better jare. The day is far spent. *A o r'ojo mu so l'okun*. I still need to get to Ota today."

"Baba, I'm serious *o*. I don't understand the *tibi* that you are talking about. Unbind me. *E tu mi nle*."

"Bode, are you serious?"

"Baba, I'm not joking *o*."

"Bode, you are starting to annoy me. Must I speak with the full complement of my mouth?"

"Baba, I honestly don't understand what you are talking about."

"I am talking about the eighty billion naira."

"Eighty billion?"

"Bode, you are misbehaving *o*. Did the judge who sent you to prison ask you to refund kobo? Look at what happened to Tafa Balogun, Lucky Igbinedion and Cecilia Ibru who all went through the injustice of having to refund a small part of their jibiti to the Nigerian State. You think your head is different from theirs? When did monkeys start boasting of a better destiny than gorillas?"

"Baba..."

"Don't baba me at all, Bode. Did Balogun, Igbinedion and Ibru offend God? No. But they were asked to refund various sums of money. Who do you think worked the miracle that allowed you to keep all of your own *tibi* and to return to it and all the interest accumulated after thirty months in prison?"

"Baba..."

"I am still talking, Bode. Who do you think worked that miracle for you? Enoch Adeboye? David Oyedepo? Chris Oyakhilome? No, my friend. Some of us pulled a lot of strings during your trial. The judge didn't wake up and allow you to keep eighty billion naira just like that."

"But Baba..."

"No need to argue any further, Bode. Here is what you will do. You will do *omoluwabi* to me with five billion naira; you will do *omoluwabi* to the Jonathan/Sambo campaign with five billion naira; you will do omoluwabi to the PDP national secretariat with five billion naira; you will earmark another five billion naira for *omoluwabi* to other deserving stakeholders, elder statesmen and chieftains of the PDP. That still leaves you sixty billion naira and interest accrued. Go and sin no more with that one."

"*Haba*, Baba, you won't even let me rest before..."

"Bode, Bode, Bode, how many times have I called you? Farida Waziri has been a very good girl since Ribadu was booted out of the EFCC. She has been a very useful girl. If you now need outsiders to explain omoluwabi to you, I can get Jonathan to activate Waziri."

"Baba, all I am trying to say is that the money is. . ."

"O-r-d-e-r-l-y!!!!!!"

"Sah!!!!!!"

"Tell the driver to get ready. We are leaving for Ota right now."

President Jonathan Attracts Foreign Investors in Rio

(June 2012)

(At the lobby of the most expensive hotel in Rio de Janeiro, overwhelmed hotel staff scurry hither and thither as they try to cope with the Nigerian delegation comprising not less than three hundred and twenty-five and a half persons. Seventy-five members of the delegation are shouting on top of their voices, insisting that hotel staff need Portuguese translations for "big man", "all protocols observed", "estacode", "Chief", "Alhaji", "advance party", "Chieftain", "Stakeholder", "First Lady", "convoy" "personal assistant" "special adviser", "senior special adviser", "special room service", "cash payment", "anticipated payment", "miscellaneous expenses", and so on and so forth, in order to provide proper service to the Nigerian delegation.

To the left, in a quiet conference room, twenty-five western business executives, led by Mr. Albert Schreiber, are seated, sipping tea, coffee, doing small talk and glancing anxiously at their Rolex wristwatches. On the conference table in front of each executive: an iPad, *a* Blackberry, The Economist *and a copy of* Wall Street Journal. *At the opposite side of the table, Ruby, Orontus, Renoks, some ministers and state governors are sweating. On the table before them: half-eaten kola nuts, bitter kola, alligator pepper, Tom Tom, and old copies of* ThisDay. *The Nigerians avoid the inquisitive gaze of the potential foreign investors.)*

"Orontus."

"Yes, Ruby boy, *wetin*?"

"*Wey oga* now, ehn? *Which kain yawa be dis*? These people are getting restless *o*. *Na we fix this meeting for 9:00 am*. This is 11:00 am and *oga still never come*."

"Hmmmm!"

"Orontus, *na hmmm you go talk*? Even the Minister of Trade and Foreign Direct Investment is not yet here. Renoks, *wey oga Trade*?"

"He needed to accompany his madam to the shopping mall this morning. I saw them when they were leaving. He promised he would be back in time for this meeting. *Maybe traffic jam catch dem*."

"Ok *o*, but what about Oga now? What do we do now? *Abi make we go check wetin dey happen for the presidential suite*?"

"Ruby."

"Yes, Orontus?"

"When you reach there, don't stop at the reception area of the presidential suite. Go inside the presidential bedroom. Check inside the sheets of the presidential bed. If you find oga there, drag him here to this meeting."

"Orontus, *you think say na joking matter be dis*? Is this the time for sarcasm?"

"Do I sound like I'm joking? *Go drag oga come now*. Luckily for you, *I hear say Nduka Obaigbena dey reorganise*, in case they don't take you back at Rutam Times when we reach home. *E be like say wetin we dey chop for Villa don tire you*. Otherwise, *which one be your own*? *Your papa name na Nigeria*? Are we not all here together waiting for oga? And you are here trying to call oga a latecomer?"

"Ehn, *e mi ke*? Call oga a latecomer? *Mewa baba mi o to be.Who born me*? I never speak words that are bigger than my mouth *o*. Orontus, please don't misunderstand me. I am not calling oga a latecomer *o*!"

"Ehen, are you trying to say that I am lying?"

"No now, Orontus, *you too dey quick vex*. I am just saying that Oga fixed this meeting for 9:00 am himself and it is now 11:00 am. And look at our foreign partners. They are getting restless. I am just saying we should at least pretend that we are doing something to get oga here. At least we can ask Renoks to go and check what is happening upstairs."

"Ruby, you will never learn the tricks of this trade. What do you think Renoks has been doing on his iPad here all morning? You think he is playing Ludo?"

"Oh, is he not just reading newspapers to keep busy while we wait for oga?"

(Orontus and Renoks explode with laughter.)

"Renoks, *abeg*, help out our friend Ruby. What are you doing on your iPad?"

"Oga Ruby, I am tweeting and also posting updates on the President's Facebook Wall about the spectacular success of this meeting with foreign investors."

"I don't understand. Which meeting?"

"Oga Ruby, *dis meeting wey we dey now*."

"I don't get it. *Dis meeting wey we never see oga*? *Dis meeting wey we never start?*"

"Oga Ruby, you are the one saying that the meeting has not started and *we never see oga*. That is not what my tweets and Facebook updates are saying."

(*Something beeps in Orontus' pocket. He springs to attention*.)

"Ah, oga is on his way *o*."

(All the Nigerians spring to attention. The CEOs look bemused. President Jonathan breezes in and the CEOs finally stand up in respect but the look on their faces betrays their irritation at the President's lateness. Two dozen aides buzz around the President as he makes his way to his designated seat. Some are carrying his papers. One is carrying his briefcase. One is carrying his cellphones. One is carrying his iPad. The President sits and invites all to sit, but only the foreign CEOs sit. The Nigerians remain standing.)

"Gentlemen, I think you are all familiar with African time? Anyway, sorry I'm late. These things happen."

(You could hear a pin drop. The foreign CEOs do not share the President's humour. Ruby winces painfully. Orontus scowls at him.)

"Anyway, we all know why we are here. Thank you for your interest in Nigeria. Before we start, I will invite two of the state governors in my delegation to each give a short welcome address."

(Each Governor takes 20 minutes to run through protocol before delivering his address. One hour later.)

"Now gentlemen, we can get down to business."

"Thank you, Mr. President; it's good that we are getting to see Nigerian culture. Can you at least ask the members of your delegation to sit down? We are not used to holding meetings with our potential partners standing up."

"Did you hear him? You people should sit down."

"Ah, Mr. President, we are all fine like this, sir. Just continue the meeting. You know oyinbo people don't understand respect for protocol and constituted authority. Just continue the meeting, sir."

"Mr. Schreiber."

"Yes, Mr. President"

"I think you heard them. My people are okay standing. How much did you say your company was thinking of investing in my country's energy sector?"

"We are looking at something in the neighbourhood of a billion dollars from now till 2015, Mr. President."

"2015? I thought you were looking at a long-term investment?"

"Yes, Mr. President. But we think it is prudent to wait and see what happens after 2015. We understand it's an election year in your country, sir. Forgive me but we did our homework. We understand that every new government cancels contracts and agreements entered into by their predecessors."

"That's correct, Mr. Schreiber. I will not lie to you. But that means you should look at working with us till 2019. We have another four years starting from 2015."

"You know the results of the 2015 elections already sir?"

(The Nigerians burst out laughing.)

"Orontus!"

"Yes, Mr. President, sir."

"Where is INEC? Go and call INEC. Tell him to come and see our foreign partners and reassure them."

(Orontus rushes out and returns with INEC. INEC gives the CEOs the desired reassurances.)

"Mr. Schreiber?"

"Yes, Mr. President."

"You just heard directly from my INEC. I travel everywhere with him because of people like you. Now that you know that I will be in office after 2015, can we get back to business?"

"Yes, Mr. President. We need a lot of concessions. We want a tax holiday for the entire duration of our operations in Nigeria. We want a 100% expatriate quota. We will need only Nigerian drivers, messengers and domestic staff for our expatriates. There are local Nigerian companies into our line of business. We expect you to do something about that, as we do not tolerate competition. We have prepared a blueprint of our investment plan for your delegation to look at, sir. If you meet our demands and conditions, we shall take care of our own special obligations to you and your designated political associates, sir. We have done our homework, sir. We know that Siemens, Halliburton and Malabu messed up while taking care of special obligations. Our approach to special obligations is Wikileaks-proof."

"Now you are talking, Mr. Schreiber. Since you understand the language of special obligations, we don't even need to see the blueprint you have prepared. When do you plan to come and start business in Nigeria?"

"Are you sure that you don't need to see the blueprint, Mr. President? We are asking for many concessions. Will your National Assembly not at least need to debate the concessions we are asking for?"

(*The Nigerians burst out laughing again*.)

"Renoks!"

"Yes, Mr. President, sir."

"I think we have some Senators in our entourage? Go and call them for me."

(Renoks dashes off and returns with two Senators.)

"My Senators."

"Yes, your Excellency, sir?"

"Our friends here are worried that you and your boys will cause problems for us. Can you please reassure them? Mr. Schreiber, these are serving Senators from my country. Please listen to them."

"*Ehem*, Mr. Schreiber, you people should not worry. You can do business with Mr. President. We will do oversight but what we see and oversee depends on what you want us to see and how Mr. President wants us to see it."

"Okay, sirs. I understand. We don't want you to see anything. I have assured Mr. President that we know how to make you not want to see anything.We will take care of our special obligations to you. We are more careful than Halliburton, Siemens and Malabu. We are Wikileaks-proof. Name where you want your special obligations deposited. Switzerland? London? Washington? Dubai? "

"In that case, welcome to Nigeria. We'll get back to you about location. Those places you mention are no longer safe havens for special obligations. Especially London. Mr. President, these are wonderful foreign investors *o*. They speak our language."

"Mr. Schreiber, now that you have been reassured by my Senators, I think you understand that you people can come and start as soon as possible. Now let us go to the second item on the agenda. Protocols of ratification and publicity of this deal in our respective countries. I think..."

(*The President is interrupted by a commotion outside the conference room. The Nigerian First Lady, accompanied by two trailer loads of aides, approaches the venue of the meeting. Orontus, Renoks and Ruby rush out to meet her.*)

"Useless people! Nonsense people! Do you know who I am? I will no longer take it from you people. The Office of the First Lady is also very important. What is he still doing at that business meeting? You people are preventing him from attending my own event. Ah, Orontus, Ruby and Renoks, you people are here too? You are part of the conspiracy?"

"No, ma."

"My friends, don't *no ma* me! You people know that Miss Brazil 2012 invited me to cut the tape and declare open her new fashion boutique today and I warned you that my husband should be by my side at the ceremony. You assured me you won't keep him long. Now, I am two hours late for my event and he is still there with those oyibo businessmen. *Abeg*, what kind of meeting are you people having? I won't leave this place until you call Ebele out for me *o*. Just imagine. NTA crew has already gone to the venue."

"But, ma…"

"Orontus, *no vex me today o*. I don't want to hear any *ma* from any of you. Just go and call Ebele for me *now now* or me and you will enter the same *trouser* today."

(Orontus rushes back to the meeting room and whispers to the President who abandons the meeting, leaving his aides to explain things to the flabbergasted foreign investors. The investors leave after being reassured that the deal is sealed.)

(Later, over beer at the hotel lobby.)

"Ruby boy."

"Yes, Orontus."

"How did oga end today's meeting?"

"He negotiated very hard and signed Memoranda of Understanding with the foreign investors on terms that are very favourable to Nigeria."

"Good. And did you see the First Lady and her aides anywhere near the venue of the meeting?"

"Which First Lady? I didn't see any First Lady anywhere near the meeting *o*. And which aides? The First Lady is here in Rio with her own aides?"

"Good. Very good, Ruby.Great answers. This is what I'm talking about. You are beginning to understand how we do it. If you don't acquire the instinct of straight-faced automatic denial, you don't belong in the Villa. You can only get better going forward."

"You think so, Orontus? It's not easy *o*, especially the part where I have to keep a straight face when saying these things."

"Trust me, Ruby, you can only get better."

"I trust you, Orontus."

Fifty Billion-Dollar Blues

(December 2013)

(Aso Rock Villa. Yoruba music-themed day in one of the expansive presidential reception rooms. Ebenezer Obey is crooning from a sophisticated sound system.)

A l'owo ma j'aiye
Eyin le mo
Awon to j'aiye l'ana da
Won t'iku won ti lo

If you have serious money
And you don't enjoy life to the hilt
That is your fucking business
Those who enjoyed life yesterday
Are dead and gone today

(General party atmosphere and genteel conversations in the ajebutter mode of the rich and powerful. Baba's raucous peals of laughter are the only throwback to unpolished bush mannerisms. In the room, the usual suspects: President Goodluck Jonathan, Mrs. Patience Jonathan, Baba Olusegun Obasanjo, General Ibrahim Babangida, General Abdulsalami Abubakar, General T.Y. Danjuma, Chief Tony Anenih, all kinds of rebel Governors, representatives of the Northern Elders' Forum, plenty of food, plenty of drinks, and assorted aides carrying the cellphones of their principals. President Jonathan can be heard above Ebenezer Obey's financial advice.)

"Ah, Baba himself! For the Baba himself! Ladies and gentlemen, it's amazing how we all here continue to owe our necks and good fortunes to Baba's quick thinking *o*!"

"Mr. President, I agree with you. You are absolutely right. I mean, look at me, I'm supposed to be *Mr. Fix It*. Yet, I was caught completely off-guard by that idiot Kano prince. But for Baba's quick action, we would all have been in a lot of trouble. I doff my hat and heart for Baba *o*!"

(*General murmur of agreement across the room.*)

"*Em*, my people, if you praise me too much, my head will swell *o*."

"Ah, Baba, let's praise you. You deserve it. You have saved the President from a very tight corner."

"Okay, praise me. It was my usual work of genius. As I sat down at the stadium in Johannesburg for Mandela's funeral, I kept thinking of the damage that this lunatic Kano prince could potentially do to our plans with his useless letter. Then I thought of the one thing that never fails to work with Nigerians: emotion. You see, no matter how grown up and educated a Nigerian is, you must always remember that his emotion never develops beyond the *Choco Milo stage* throughout his or her life. Give children Choco Milo and you can divert their attention away from anything. I knew instantly that a letter containing more sensational tsunami than that of the Kano prince would divert their attention from our money. Throwing Nigerians Choco Milo worked for those who ruled them before us; throwing Nigerians Choco Milo has worked for us since we started ruling them; throwing Nigerians Choco Milo will work for our children who will rule Nigerians when we are dead and buried."

(*Thunderous applause in the room.*)

"*Em*, Your Excellency President Jonathan."

"Yes, my dear General IBB."

"Well, now that Baba has mentioned our money, I think it is time to get down to business. I still need to be in Minna today to receive another APC delegation. You know that those fools literally sleep on my verandah these days."

"Ah, yes, you're right, General. Gentlemen, the meeting is about to start. If you are not supposed to be here, please exit now."

(*All aides exit. Patience Jonathan remains seated, beaming. Baba whispers into President Jonathan's ear.*)

"*Em*, Jona, your madam is still here now."

"Yes now, Baba, I can see her."

"*Haba*, don't you understand? Tell her to go out too now."

"*Ehn*, Baba, you want to kill me? Tell Patience to go out? Baba, leave matter, she is the real President *o*."

"Ah, Jona, *wo aiye e nta*! See your life! Okay, let me help you get her out of here."

"Ah, Baba, please I beg you, leave her alone *o*."

(*Too late. Baba is already approaching the First Lady.*)

"My one and only Madam *Peshe*!"

"Baba, you are our father."

"Peshe, Peshe! The lioness of Okrika! May Soponna strike any other woman who looks at Jona."

"Baba, we thank God. We thank you."

"*Ehen*, Madam Peshe, *shebi* you know that whenever I'm here in the Villa, I will only eat what you personally cook because I am yet to see any woman who cooks soup like you in the whole of Africa."

"Ah, Baba, you are flattering me again *o*."

"It is not flattery *o*, Madam Peshe. This one that you are sitting here with us, it means you want me to eat food cooked by Villa cooks today?"

"Ah, Baba! Okay, let me leave you men alone and go and personally cook your own meal."

"That is what I'm talking about my daughter. Thank you. O *kare omobinrin yi*."

(*The First Lady exits.*)

"Ah, Baba, how did you do it?"

"Leave me alone *jare*, Jona. *O ti de ju*. Must I teach you everything including how to flatter a woman to get her to do anything you want? Start the meeting *jare*."

"Ladies and gentlemen, we are all here to review Operation Fifty-Billion-Dollars-For-2015. Now that Baba, through a stroke of genius, has been able to divert the country's attention away from the money and to his letter, we have to move quickly and discuss the sharing formula."

"Your Excellency?"

"Yes, Mr. Fix It."

"First, I want to congratulate you for raising the fifty billion dollars."

"I didn't raise it *o*. *Nne* One and *Nne* Two did it. I only provided Presidential leverage."

"Ah, Jona."

"Yes, Baba?"

"Sorry for interrupting you, but how do you go about picking those your *Nnes*? One bought bulletproof BMWs for some cool dollars and another two have raised fifty billion dollars for 2015. Anyway, Mr. Fix It, you have no mouth to congratulate anybody *o*. When we put you in Works, how much were you able to raise? Now ordinary women have raised fifty billion dollars and you are talking. You should be ashamed of yourself."

"Baba, please let's stay on point. General IBB, your opinion?"

"Well, President Jonathan, have you determined the traditional courtesy cut for us the elder statesmen here? How much is going to Baba, General Danjuma, General Abdulsalami, and I? And since General Integrity will never attend these meetings and will reject his share if we send it to him, we can add it to ours. So, as usual, we take our cut first and decide how to disburse the rest for 2015."

"Yes, General IBB, in view of all the contending issues, I have fixed the traditional courtesy cut for you elders at ten billion dollars. As usual, you will work out the sharing formula among yourselves. We are left with a balance of forty billion dollars. Baba, I hope that works for you?"

"Jona, you know by now that no amount of money works for me, but let me not be an *agbaya*. Let me agree this time. Now let's move on to these noisemakers in the Northern Elders' Forum. General Abubakar should handle that side."

(*General Abubakar turns to the representatives of the Northern Elders' Forum and speaks.*)

"Folks, I'm a man of few words. Four years of waiting is nothing if you are busy investing ten billion dollars. Take ten billion dollars and bury your agitation for the Presidency to shift to the North in 2015. You don't have to openly work for President Jonathan. Just go and get busy investing your share of the ten billion dollars and disappear from circulation. Remember that if you refuse to take this money, he has the might of the Nigerian state and will still rig that election anyway. Guys, grow a brain. Don't lose both ways. Take ten billion dollars and advise the North to wait for 2019."

"Okay, General Abdulsalami, we hear you. But this ten billion is for how many of us? Can the President add three oil blocks to it?"

"Alhaji, don't push it. Ten billion and nothing more. It's dollars *o*. The sharing formula is for you, members of the executive of the Northern Elders Forum, to decide when you get back to Kaduna."

"Okay. We agree."

"Your Excellency."

"Yes, General Abdulsalami?"

"We have the North. Ten billion dollars."

"Okay. Baba, *shey* you hear. We are down to thirty billion dollars."

"*Ehen*, these rebel rascals, there are seven or eight of them?"

"Well, Baba, they are all here but I don't know in what combination. They were seven. Then they were five and two, and then they were five and one and one. But we have seven of them here."

"Jona!"

"Yes, Baba?"

"Give them one billion each and let them go and *sempe*."

"*Sempe*?"

"Cool temper."

"Ah, okay. That makes seven billion dollars. But Lamido already cornered ten billion naira through his sons. Should he also get a billion dollars?"

"Jona, give those boys what I said. By the way, where is Rotimi? Rotimi! Rotimi!"

(*Rotimi approaches the centre of the room and kneels down. Baba addresses him.*)

"*Ehen*, Rotimi, your drama has gone on long enough."

"Yes, I know, Baba."

"You will leave this meeting with one billion dollars. The money is to organise your campaign for the Senate in 2015. Once you leave this meeting, go back to Port Harcourt and engineer how to lose your ongoing battle with the Presidency. You understand that the Presidency must not be seen to have lost out in a battle with a governor."

"I understand, Baba."

"Okay, Jona, what else do you have for Rotimi?"

"In addition to the one billion dollars, he gets two oil blocks. He gets to continue his association openly with APC but must come back to us once he is elected to the Senate."

"Rotimi, *shey* you hear President Jonathan. Do you agree?"

"I agree, Baba."

"Okay, go and arrange how Bipi will impeach you. Protest a little and disappear into APC. See you at the Senate in 2015. Jona, where are we?"

"Well, Baba, ten billion for elder statesmen, ten billion for the Northern Elders Forum, seven billion for the rebels. That's twenty-seven billion dollars."

"Okay, we must earmark ten billion dollars for Bode George now that he is completely free to work for us again."

"Haba Baba! Ten billion dollars for Bode George?"

"Jona, I think you are underestimating the importance of Lagos. Until we take that state, we cannot really say that we own Nigeria, even if you win in 2015. You understand that the owner of the treasury of that state is singlehandedly financing APC and poking his rude finger in our noses all the time just because he owns that treasury? Whatever we do, we have to capture that treasury. Capturing the treasury of Lagos state is a do-or-die affair."

"But Baba, we can always fly him here in the dead of night and cut another deal."

"That will be another temporary solution. Bode is the only stormy petrel capable of handling him. But Bode needs money."

"But Baba, what will ten billion dollars do? Do you know how much the man rakes in monthly from that treasury he owns in Lagos? Lamorde showed me his file last week and I nearly had a heart attack."

"That is why you will give Bode five oil blocks in addition to the ten billion dollar mobilisation fee. Besides, something will work for us. Sooner or later, the people of Lagos will get tired of their money being used to build a personal empire across the southwest. They will begin to insist that the money for Lagos must be spent exclusively on the development of Lagos. Once that happens, we move in for the kill."

"Okay, Baba, ten billion for Bode George. So, we have run through thirty-seven billion dollars. What about *Nne* One and *Nne* Two? Without the extraordinary work of those two women, we won't be here."

"Ah, yes, they tried. Encourage them with $1.5 billion each."

"That's three billion dollars. We are at forty billion dollars."

"I think the whole house here would agree that the remaining ten billion dollars should be disbursed at your discretion, Mr. President."

(*Outside the room, some eavesdropping disgruntled aides whisper.*)

"*Chei*, Ruby."

"Wetin now, Renoks?"

"You no hear? The money don remain ten billion dollars *o*."

"*Ehen*?"

"What do you mean ehen?"

"They have not mentioned aides now. And the money don nearly finish. It takes billions to effectively monitor social media these days…"

"*Haba*, Renoks!"

"*Wetin now*, Oga Doyin, was I talking to you? I was talking to Oga Ruby."

"*Ole ni e*. You are a thief. No respect for elders. Elders are sharing money that will guarantee your future here beyond 2015 and you are doing *longa throat. Foolish boy*."

"At least nobody in Benue and Imo states has accused me of contract *jibiti*."

"*Ehn*, Renoks, are you talking to me? Ruby, you are here and this small boy is insulting me? I will…"

(*Madam Peshe's voice screaming from the kitchen interrupts him.*)

"Renoks! Ruby! Doyin! Where are these boys when you need them? Renoks! Ruby! Doyin! Have you set the table?"

They all roar, "Yes Madam!" and rush to the kitchen.

THE END

29819059R00131

Made in the USA
San Bernardino, CA
18 March 2019